W9-BDD-546

Prophecy, part 1

Translation: Kumar Sivasubramanian
Production: Grace Lu
Nicole Dochych
Anthony Quintessenza

Copyright © 2012 Tetsuya Tsutsui / Ki-oon
All rights reserved.
First published in France in 2012 by Ki-oon,
an imprint of AC Media Ltd.
English translation rights arranged through
Tuttle-Mori Agency, Inc.
English language version produced by Vertical, Inc.

Translation provided by Vertical Comics, 2014
Published by Vertical Comics, an imprint of
Vertical, Inc., New York

This is a work of fiction.

ISBN: 978-1-939130-59-4

Manufactured in the United States of America

First Edition

Second Printing

Vertical, Inc.
451 Park Avenue South
7th Floor
New York, NY 10016
www.vertical-inc.com

The War Begins!
So Does A Friendship!
© Felipe Smit

TETSUYA TSUTSUI

PROPHECY

01

CONTENTS

File001 3

File002 37

File003 69

File004 97

File005 131

File006 163

File007 190

his is a work of
on. Any resemblance
ersons, groups, or
nts is purely coincidental.

File
001

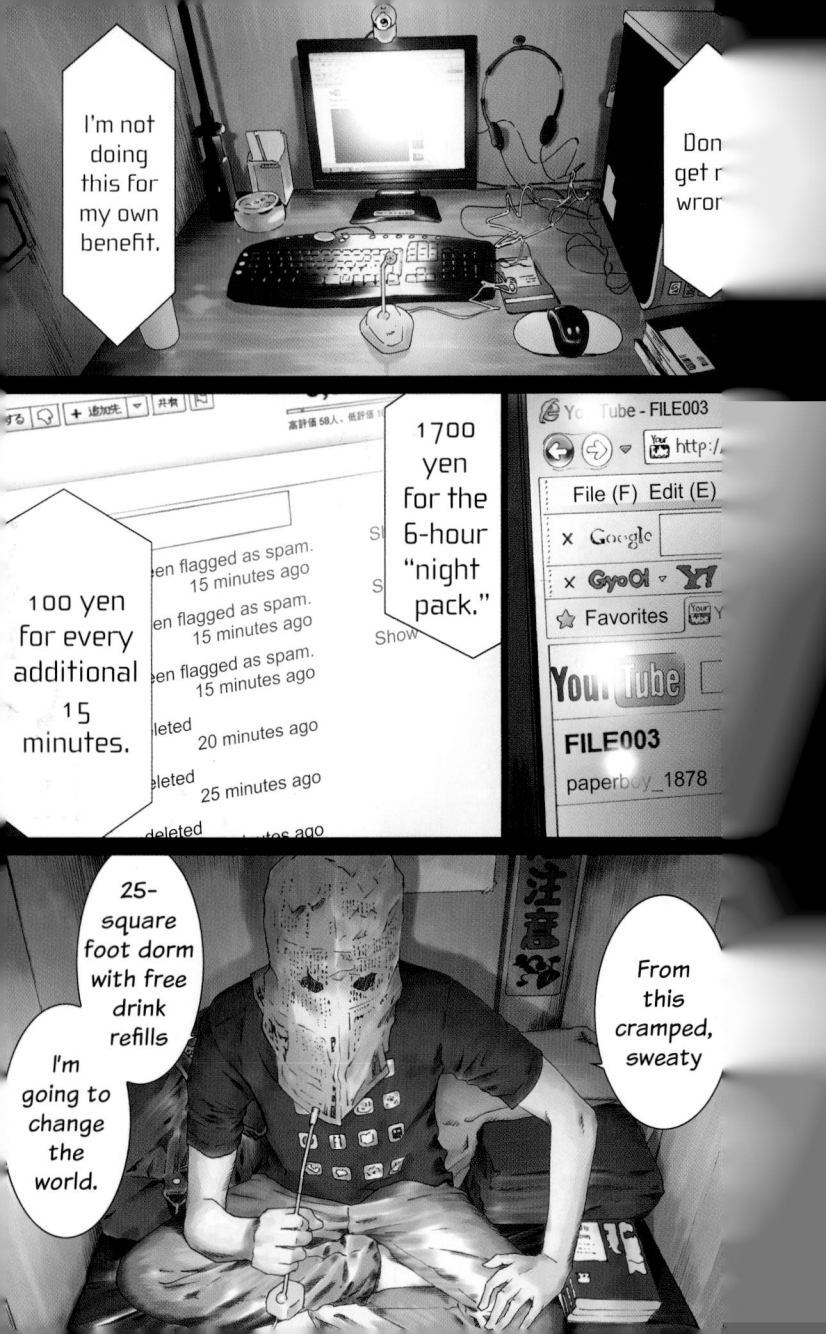
I'm not doing this for my own benefit.
Don get r wror
1700 yen for the 6-hour "night pack."
100 yen for every additional 15 minutes.
en flagged as spam. 15 minutes ago
en flagged as spam. 15 minutes ago
en flagged as spam. 15 minutes ago
leted 20 minutes ago
eleted 25 minutes ago
deleted
Show
Tube - FILE003
http:/
File (F) Edit (E)
Google
GyoOi
Favorites
FILE003
paperboy_1878
25-square foot dorm with free drink refills
I'm going to change the world.
From this cramped, sweaty

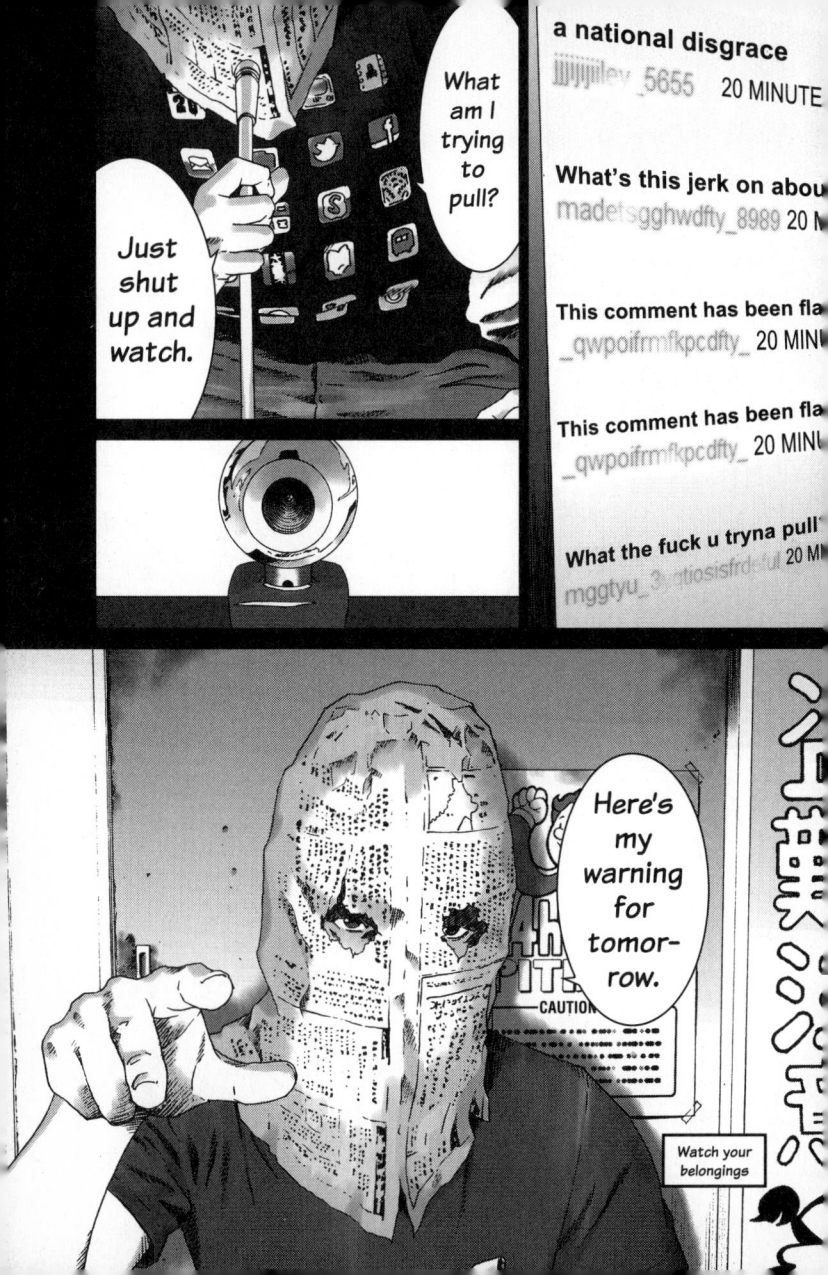
What am I trying to pull?
Just shut up and watch.
a national disgrace
20 MINUTE
What's this jerk on abou
20 M
This comment has been fla
qwpoifrmfkpcdfty 20 MIN
This comment has been fla
qwpoifrmfkpcdfty 20 MIN
What the fuck u tryna pull
20 M
Here's my warning for tomor-row.
CAUTION
Watch your belongings

May 21, 10:00
U CITY, TOCHIGI PREFECTURE

Whoa, incredible.

So the suspect's in junior high?

Yup.

Illegally uploaded games, some 10 billion yen in damages.

Oh?
They're from a section just formed this year.
A unit specializing in internet crime.
Say, those detectives before.
They had Metro PD armbands.

Ah, they've got a Wikipedia page.
The unit name is...

The Cyber Force's role is like surveillance over the internet.
These guys are a team of specialists on cyber crimes.

But wasn't there already some unit like that?
Cyber Force or something.

IT'S THE SAME DAMN THING!
6-16
MASUYAMA
Anti Cyber Crimes Division ...

TOCHIGI PREFECTURAL POLICE
VIBRATE

Seize all of it, please.
Mobile game devices, computers, external storage devices.
Sir !

KSHIK
KSHIK

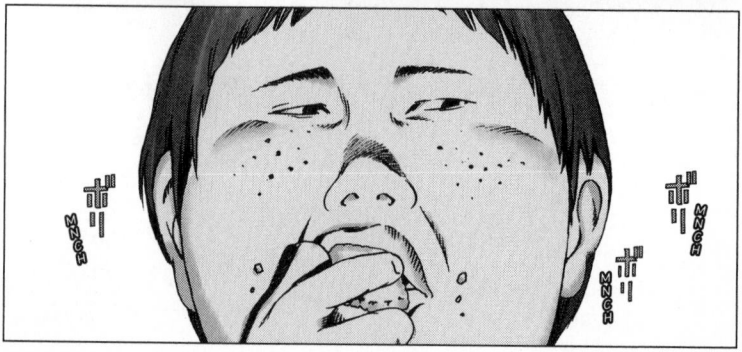
KZOKZ
KZOKZ
KZOKZ
KZOKZ

SWIPE
TAP
twitter
SMILE
SMILE
Close
New Tweet
@genius_masuyan
BEEP
HOUSE SEARCH LIVE!
KA
KLIK
Cool it with the photos.
Hey, kid.

Illegally uploading game software.
That's a violation of copyright law.
Metropolitan Police Department
Anti Cyber Crimes Division
ERIKA YOSHINO
Shota Masu-yama.
You do realize you're a suspect, right ?
Specifically, Article 23 of the Copyright Act:
Infringe-ment of author's public trans-mission rights.
"Don't rip game data without permission and release it to the world, you complete jackass."
Put simply, it says...

A game copier.
Yeah.
This is one of those things?
Hey, Ichikawa.
Same Division
MANABU ICHIKAWA
Same Division
DAIKI OKAMOTO
Oh.
DROP

They say gaming companies have lost major bucks because of them.
But unscrupulous people started using them to extract the game software data and spread it on the internet.
It was originally a component for making backups of game software.
R4

Hmf.
Damn, kids these days...

Thanks to pressure from the Ministry of Finance, importing copiers is already banned,
but with more than a million already sold, the situation's totally out of hand.

Roughly 45 billion yen in damages
caused by downloads from your site.
But you got loads of "pin money," didn't you?
SHIK
Huh ?
What're ya talkin' about?
I didn't get no cash! I didn't steal nothin'!

Your blog is totally plastered
with affiliate ads.
Th...
THAT...
My readers just send me stuff on their own!
I-I do this as a volunteer!
And you got all these.
KLATTER
That's right! A volun-teer!
I adver-tize their games for them!
A volun-teer.

The swine's blabbing ...
THERE ARE PLENTY OF GAMES LIKE THAT, WHERE WORD-OF-MOUTH MADE 'EM HITS, RIGHT?
IF THE GAME'S ANY GOOD, CUSTOMERS'LL HAPPILY PAY MONEY TO BUY IT!

It's the stupid game company's fault for making a crappy game!!
If a game's sales go down
that ain't my fault!

WHY THE HELL DO THE COPS GOTTA DO WHATEVER THE SHITTY GAME MAKERS SAY?!
LIKE I SAID!! THAT'S TOTALLY WRONG !!
CRASH!

What you say may be quite true,
but when a game company actually files a complaint ...
we can't just sit on our hands, now, can we?

That's why domestic games are quickly gettin' left in the dust by foreign companies!
Gettin' stingy over their fuckin' rights over stuff like this!

Japanese games have totally jumped the damn shark!
They got so much free time, go make a decent fuckin' game!

He means stuff that's lost its appeal.
... Shark ?
Ichi-ka-wa.

THIS IS THE VOICE OF THE PEOPLE!
I-I know! My Twitter!
Any second now, tons of replies backing me up are gonna flood in. Watch this!!

There's no way copying a game for private use is illegal.
For sure, there are restrictions on importing copiers,
but owning one isn't a problem.
You know a lot.
If this new anti internet crime squad is hunting down minors with copiers ...
Well, to be honest, I think they're over-stepping.
My kid's got one.
Pestered me for it for his birthday.
Yeah, I hear they're real popular with kids now.
Rumor has it even National Diet MPs let their own families use them!
Ha ha ha!
No way !
This seems to be the suspect's Twitter account.
Ooh !
Well, that was fast.
Let's see ...
Oh.
Here we go!

Why, they're treating you just like a god. Look at all these tributes pouring in.
Satisfying, was it?
Everyone's just flip-flopped, and now they're laughing at you. How's that feel?
...
@genius_masu
LMFAO
LMFAO.
@genius_r
u deser
@genius
Copie
You deserve it.
@geniu
(^Д^) Gah
Copier freak arrested. Schadenfreude FTW.
us_masuyar
lolz
Gah ...
Repe
@genius_
d it c
Take that.
Repent in juvie, you little shit.
ius_masu
igation
genius_masu

Seems like some people have the wrong idea. But don't worry.
Ung ... gh ...!
Uuuhh...
Why... those jerks ...
... Shit ...!
No one's going to ship you off to juvie or a reformatory.
However, I would like to express one opinion, if I may.
I'D LOVE TO NAB EVERY LITTLE SNOT LIKE YOU,
TOSS YOU INTO A CELL
AND BEAT YOU UNTIL YOU TWISTED BASTARDS GOT STRAIGHT-ENED OUT!

PAT
You'll be getting a damage claim from the game company and a court-issued subpoena shortly.
Best have a talk with your parents about how to pay for it.
45 billion yen.

So hang in there, kid!
Well, you'll probably need about 10 lifetimes to earn enough.

WHU
MP

Move! Make way!
Could we have a statement, please?
Come on, don't push!
A com-ment, sir!

Do you have any comment on that?
Some people are criticizing the tactic of unmasking minors for use as object lessons!
(No one's actually said this)

SLAM
A state-ment, please !!

Since starting this job
there's one lesson I've learned well.
The level of idiocy of some people in this world surpasses imagination.
Sheesh.
She's pretty frosty, eh.
But she sure is pretty!

Oh ho.
Erika Yoshi-no.
Seems that woman was a lieutenant, age 26.
So that was that cyber-something squad, huh?
Anti Cyber Crimes Division.
Though I wonder if a lady like her is cut out for it.
Sounds pretty fast to me.
Lieutenant at 26? Quite a feat!
But she sure is pretty ...
Haha !
In that case she was a bit too surly, wasn't she?
Been lots of cop scandals lately.
Maybe they're trying to charm the media?

May 21, 13:30

K CITY, ISHIKAWA PREFECTURE

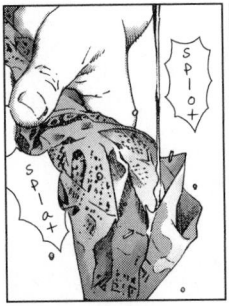

VWOOSH
...
VROOOOOM

TRAFFIC ACCIDENTS (YESTERDAY)
DEATHS
May 21, 13:30
TOKYO METROPOLITAN POLICE DEPARTMENT
METROPOLITAN POLICE DEPARTMENT ANTI CYBER CRIMES DIVISION
INVESTIGATION SQUAD 2
INVESTIGATION SQUAD 3
INVESTIGATION SQUAD 4
SOPHISTICATED INFORMATION TECHNOLOGY CRIMES MANAGEMENT OFFICE
Ah!
Lieu-tenant Yoshi-no!
Cyber Force is calling for you!
KA
KLATCH

Weird videos on Yourtube ?

This is the third one.
Similar videos repeatedly get posted then deleted.
They started attracting traffic a few days ago.

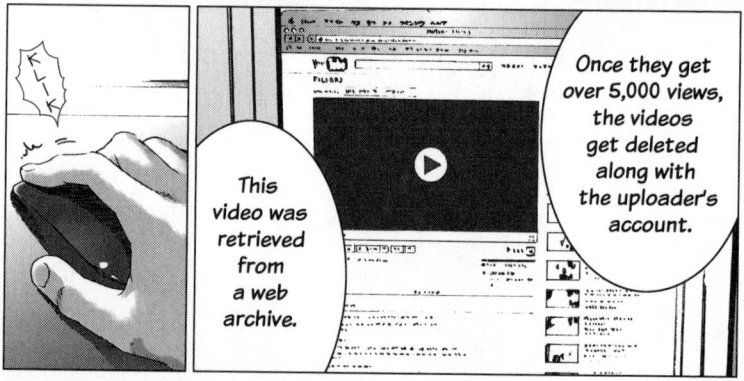
KLIK
This video was retrieved from a web archive.
Once they get over 5,000 views, the videos get deleted along with the uploader's account.

Here's my warning for tomorrow.
CAUTION

The target is a certain food processor that caused
a mass food poisoning incident last month.

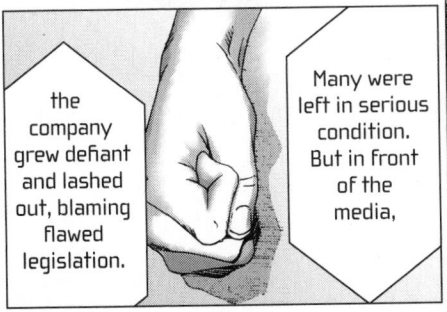
Many were left in serious condition. But in front of the media,
the company grew defiant and lashed out, blaming flawed legislation.

I'm gonna cook them until they're well-done.
I hereby sentence these screwups.
Since they don't know how to handle food properly,
The hell was that ...?
HUSH...

The poster's username was paperboy_1878.
paperboy_187
He seems to keep reopening his account
with a different number after the underscore each time.

Yes. It's definitely a match.
He might be trying to show he didn't record this ages ago.
Sort of like a time stamp.
I see.

That newspaper he had over his head.
That layout was from yesterday's morning edition, right?

Can you work out the location of the computer that he posted from?
Well ...
Analysis of the IP address will take a while...
Probably within the Kanto region.
Either Kanagawa or Saitama, I figure.

The poster in the background of the video.
Ichikawa.
They've only got locations in Tokyo, Kanagawa, and Saitama.
That's the character mascot of a chain of internet cafés called Pit Boy.
Why do you say that?
If you wanted to post a video like this,
it's only natural that you'd think to avoid locations in Tokyo, right?
In Tokyo we have a municipal bylaw that requires users to present ID when using net cafés.
For now we'd better check out all the Pit Boy branches.
But if this poster is just a fake, then all that means nothing.
I see.
So that leaves Kanagawa or Saitama.

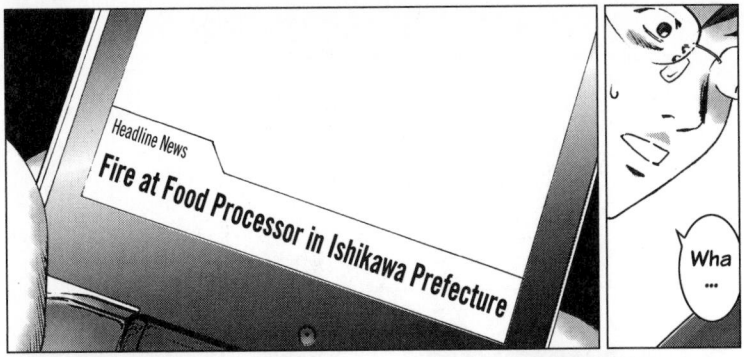
Headline News
Fire at Food Processor in Ishikawa Prefecture
Wha ...

There's a TV crew... just happens to be on the scene...
Says they're broad-casting live...

What's up?
Fire...
at a food processor in Ishikawa ...

still not ...
Zzz...
Buffering...
Fire trucks ...!
Zzz...
Hurry ...!!

I'll connect to Iseg TV.

As you can see!
The entire area is covered ...

koff
koff!
covered in pitch black smoke !!

Run! Run away!
Whoa, whoa... it can't be...
That newspaper guy...?

NOW HE'S GONE AND DONE IT.
HMF.

Wasn't that him?!
Aah !
It's him !
Oka-moto !
Just now, for a second ...
In the crowd of onlookers ...!
Aah ...!
Hey, Ichi-kawa !
Can you record this video?
Oh... Yeah !
Al-ready on it!

SO HERE WE HAVE
KRIK
ゴキ
KRAK
ゴキ
ANOTHER LITTLE MORON ...

File
002
FSSHHH
JIKE
JIKE
whisk
whisk
whisk
whisk
...

GRUB'S ALMOST READY.
HUNGRY ?
WHSK
WHSK
File 002

Mmf!
Mrrmm!
KLAK
Whoa, there.
HISS
Don't rush me now.
You wanted this, didn't you?
I'll let you have it soon enough ...
Nnff!
Ffm!
HISS

Let's have a quick look at the other two videos.
This "Paperboy" has posted three videos in total.
May 21, 14:15
METROPOLITAN POLICE DEPARTMENT CONFERENCE ROOM 3
That's about two weeks ago.
"FILE001" was posted on May 6 at 20:40.
The file names are "FILE001" and "FILE002" respectively.
A simple sequential system.
Here's my warning for tomorrow.

DIARY
PHOTOS
SAN'S DIARY
<< PREVIOUS PAGE
When he announced it on an SNS, people instantly ganged up on him.
Four years ago, he devised a creative new dish: cockroaches deep-fried in the cooker at his restaurant.
The target this time is a former part-timer at a certain restaurant.
Shuya Fujiki.
See more photos
Shuya Fujiki (92)
Last login within 45)
But I highly applaud the drive to discover gourmet delights even at risk to one's life.
Rumor has it he even dropped out of high school because of this fracas.
I SHALL FILL HIM UP WITH MY OWN SPECIALLY-PREPARED MENU.
I HAVE A REWARD FOR THE LITTLE GOURMAND.

There was definitely such a commotion four years ago.
The flame war was even covered by national newspapers.
You gotta be kidding me.
On the internet, if you post something that's just meant as a prank
it often escalates into an out-of-control commotion.
And if you post on an SNS, people can instantly discover your identity.
After that incident, the restaurant where he worked and their HQ were deluged with irate phone calls, and some called for a boycott.
In the end the company published an apology statement on their website and that apparently resolved the matter.
I just ...
My head hurts.
I don't get it.

So in the end what came of this threat?
Apparently a video of the punishment was transmitted online via streaming video,
but there's no trace of it now.
Whoa! Miss-ing?
I hope he's OK.
The targeted student has not been in contact with his parents
and it would seem he's missing.
Let's look at "FILE 002."
Here's my warning for tomorrow.

earlier this year, which caused quite a commotion.
He tweeted this, in regards to a sex crime committed by a fellow student
The target this time is a former student of R University:
Shuji Seki.
"You reap what you sow, amirite?"
"It's the woman's fault for being so easy."
I'LL INJECT HIM WITH A VERY SPECIAL SPIRIT BOMB!
HOW WONDERFUL THAT HE'S GOT SUCH SPIRIT!

Posting time was May 13, 22:10.
This erupted into a flame war on Twitter this year
sparked by tweets defending a man suspected of raping a woman at R University.
Here, too, the target's identity was discovered via SNS,
his home phone number
plus the clubs he was in
even a tentative job offer.

In this case, too, his potential employer ended up inundated with irate calls and appeals for a boycott.
Rumors say that the target's job offer was eventually retracted, probably as a consequence.

Something I don't quite understand.
What do you mean "flame war"?
Basically a net lynching.
People make antisocial comments or the like online
and so many attacks flood in that the situation gets out of hand.

People post indiscreet opinions on Twitter or their blogs,
then people work out their identity through SNSs or their profile page.
They find their address, people sneak photos of their homes and post them online.
They lodge complaints with their employers and call for boycotts of their products.
That's the standard pattern of these flame wars.
What I don't quite get is
if you don't like what someone posted, why not just tell them directly?
Why go so far as to boycott his employer ?
'cause they're not satisfied just slamming the culprit.
Lot of people with too much time on their hands.
They brandish a warped sense of justice. They'd stone a drowning man to death.
I think the number of people who think that's a fun pastime are on the rise.

Can we get in touch with the second one, Shuji Seki?
Here's his address.
Seems he hasn't moved yet.
It's in Tokyo. You might be able to see him if you leave now.

... Spirit Bombs ...

If he's had contact with our criminal, we might get a statement.
And find out what "Spirit Bombs" are.

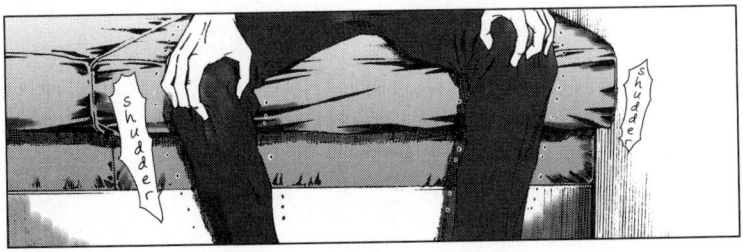
Shudder
Shudder

What do the cops want with me now?
Mr. Seki.
You were recently kid-napped?
We'd like you to tell us what hap-pened.
I week ago, I was leaving my job.
This odd, chubby man called out to me.
He said he was a lawyer,
but he didn't seem like he made much money.
And he looked wicked suspi-cious.
But he said he specialized in internet defamation cases or something
and that's what's troubling me, so ...
I figured I'd at least hear him out.

But as I was getting into the car
I was sud-denly hit from behind.
When I came to, I was tied up, naked, in an abandoned old building.
And that's where I was as-saulted.
What about the man's age and height?
Height... about 5'5".
Maybe in his mid-30's.
I... uhm...
Y- You're a wo-man...
I'm a detec-tive.
Stop fretting and tell me.
... OK.
How were you assault-ed,
ex-act-ly?
Well...
He used, uhm...
He had a s-sex toy, and he...
From behind he...

YOU'RE SAYING HE SHOVED A VIBRATOR UP YOUR ASS.
KLANK
...
WHISPER
WHISPER
...
Language like that doesn't really shock me.
I'm not a child.
Is that the issue?
WIPE
WIPE
Geez, this lady ...

So not only
do the police not protect me,
you've come here to ridicule me instead?
We have no intention of the kind.
Day in, day out, the harassing phone calls never end.
Somebody always tails me from the shadows
smirking and taking photos with their phone.
DO YOU GET AT ALL WHAT THAT FEELS LIKE?!
And after all that I'm abducted and tied up!
Did I really do anything that bad?!

YOU REAP WHAT YOU SOW, AM I RIGHT?
BUT YOU WENT ALONG SO EASILY, DIDN'T YOU?

...!
What do you think about those words now?

I'm leaving.
Wait a minute.

WH
AM

Oh, now.
Only joking!

Did he maybe have some padding around his stomach?
Did it seem like that to you?
Something you said before
about him being a "chubby man" is bothering me.

Are we done here?
His arms were fat, too.
If there was anything artificial like that, I'd have noticed.

Thank you very much!
We appreciate your cooperation!

Unconsciously covering his rear...
Sure musta hurt...
Thank you for coming!
トッコ
BOB

VVRRR
I definitely feel it's off to call this guy's body type "chubby."
Perhaps we should assume that there are multiple "Paperboys"?
I don't think that's possible.
If they were after money, that's one thing.
But multiple full-fledged adults involved in these messed-up crimes? Well...
Well, right now we don't have a clincher
either way...

Ichikawa.
Lend me your iPad.
Sure.
トーンッ TAP
For example, if a skinny person looks at an average body type, he might feel they're "chubby."
There are plenty of cases of biased perspectives causing erroneous witness statements.

Video "FILE003" was posted on the 20th at 11:40 p.m.
If it was posted from the Kanto region,
if you got to Shin-Yokohama Station the next day by 6 a.m., you could arrive at K City in Ishikawa Prefecture before noon.
You could also reach the site of the arson at 1:00 p.m.

So a single person could pull it off?
They'd be very rushed.
What about the man's height?
In the news footage he looked to be about 5'11"...

In that news footage, going by the size of the vending machine behind him,
from that camera angle, the man had to be at least 5'9".
That's still just an inference.
If he was standing on some sort of platform for a better view, that's the end of that.
All we can say at this stage is a lone wolf or multiple criminals are both possible.
You're right ...
RIRIRIRING
Yoshino speaking.
... Yes.
Uh huh.
... I see.
Got it.

Pit Boy, A City branch, booth 24, with a reclining seat.
The location of the computer used to upload "FILE003."
The IP was traced to Kanagawa Prefecture.
He may indeed have consciously avoided Tokyo locations.
Ichi-ka-wa.
Your deduction was right.
What do you mean ?
...
I-chi-ka-wa.
So you wanna pay them a visit before we head back to HQ?
Yes.
Would you mind?
You really are surprisingly transparent.
That's not true...

May 21, 16:30
A CITY, KANAGAWA PREFECTURE

But it's so strange ...
Until the next morning, booth 24 was vacant the whole time.
Ah, I see. There is indeed evidence that the computer in booth 24 was in use from about 11:30 p.m. on the 20th.
Vacant ?
We have security camera footage, too.
We can't actually see inside the booths, but we can check when people come in and out.
Let's fast forward from the afternoon of the 20th and see.
SSSS
Hmm ...
Seems to be no one coming or going.

Which means there are two conceivable methods:
Is it possible someone could have prepared beforehand an automated script to upload the video?
That's hard to imagine.
The computers here are completely rebooted and initialized after every use.
One: He comes into the café as an ordinary user,
waits until a time when the booth in question is empty then goes in.
After posting the video, he leaves the booth.
Then by some means, he swaps out the security camera footage.
Or two: He infiltrates Pit Boy's intracompany network from an outside location,
then remotely operates the computer in the empty booth via remote login to post the video.

It would be technically impossible for the footage to be tampered with after the fact.
The security camera footage is also sent to the company that's entrusted with our security system.
Hmm ...
To be honest, those would both be difficult.
I think it would be even more difficult for someone outside to infiltrate our intracompany network.
As for the other one, a person off-site logging in remotely.
doesn't sound beyond the range of any geek with a bit of know-how.
I wonder.
Taking remote control of a PC in a net café

Popular Com
Death Th
Tokyo In
After that, HQ completely overhauled our security systems.
Much to our shame, it ended up making a TV news program.
Well, about 3 years ago, there was some-one who sent death threats to a celebrity from one of our locations.
We can't allow external users to hack into the classified servers that hold our intranet and customer information.
That's why we have these now.
What is that?
It's called an "OTP Token."
An OTP is a One-Time Password, generated for single use only.
The token is a physical authen-tication device.

So, who carries these?
Only the managers of each Pit Boy branch
and the staff at the head office.
A hash function-generated one-time password ...
Certainly not an easy thing to break through.
I really think we're
the only net café that has taken their security this far.
But is it still possible that someone could get through?
Even an expert hacker using a supercomputer wouldn't be able to unlock it in time.
I mean, that's what the security company asserts, anyways.
I see...

But we've received no such report at all about this incident.
And if any attempt was made to hack in
we would certainly be notified by the security center.
Which limits it to the branch managers and the head office personnel ...
In-deed.
I don't grasp all of it, but
does that mean only an insider could have posted the video?
Oh, erm ...
... Huh ?

Mr. Yasuda.
Are you dissatisfied with how the company treats you?
Huh ...?
Would you mind coming down to the station for a quick chat?
Whaaa?!

SLAM
BAM

BBRRRMM
ブロロロロ

ニノヤッ!!
SKFF
... The cops.
Faster than I'd expected.
le coq sp

PROPHECY

File
003

WHIRRR
WELCOME
W'lcome !

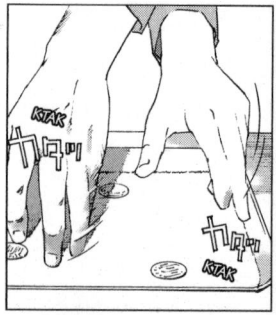
KTAK
KTAK
KTAK

...?

300 yen is your change.
...Thanks.

Night pack. Re-cliner.
1700 yen.
He reeks ...

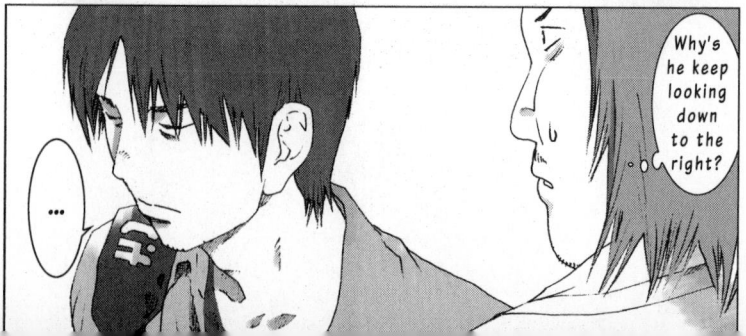
Why's he keep looking down to the right?
...

Low-malt beer, 105 yen...
Night pack, 1700 yen.
Fried chicken, 180 yen.
Reclining Seat Booth No. 12

shrrip shrrip
...

Just enough to scrape by today.

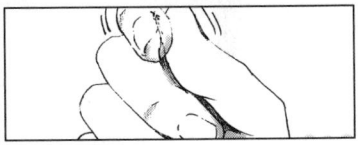

Guess I'll shower ...
Shower (10 minutes): 200 yen
Bath Towel (loan): 150 yen
Shampoo & Conditioner: 50 yen
Tooth Brush Set: 100 yen

SNFFF…
SNFFF…

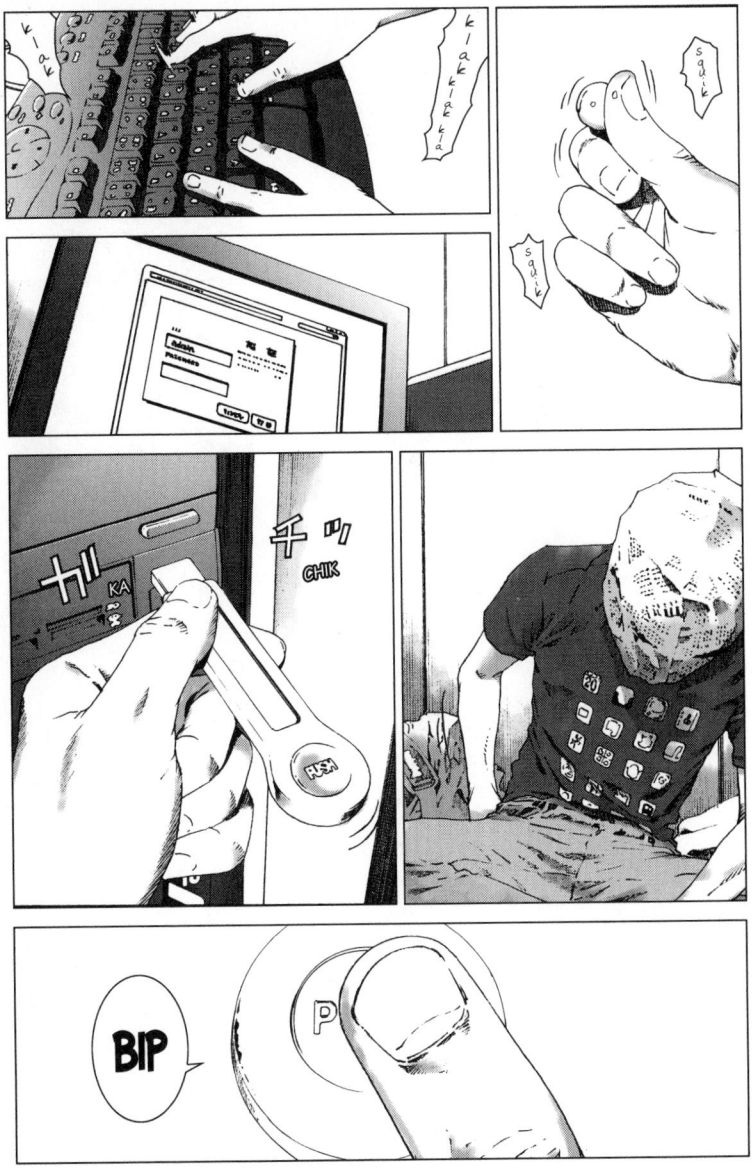
kiak kiak kia
kiak
squik
squik
LOGIN
PASSWORD
LOGIN
カード
KA
チッ
CHIK
BIP
P

PING
ACCEPTED!
BLINK
Now to search for an empty booth
KRAK
in one of the 12 branches in Kanagawa and Saitama.
How about this one today?
#8 recliner booth, W City branch, Saitama.
KLIK

May 22, 18:10
TOKYO METROPOLITAN POLICE DEPARTMENT
Yasuda, the manager, is clean.
We looked into the part-time staff, too, but it seems the chance of someone on the inside being involved is slim.
I see.
Gotta write up a formal apology again.
カチャッ
KACHAK
Whew ...
I made inquiries with Pit Boy's head office as well,
but there've been no reports of any OTP tokens being stolen from any branches.
I see ...
Good work.

Mean-ing?
It's begun to spread.
We still don't know how he posted the videos
but we should set aside that mystery and switch to realistic counter-measures.

2CHAN NEWS FLASH ROUNDUP
This is a news aggregator blog that gets over 2 million pageviews per day.

There's an article about Paperboy at the top.

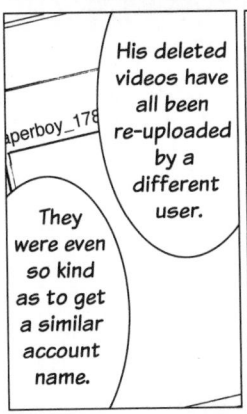

This comment has been flagged a

Cops, do your fucking jobs! lol

cyber police () haha

This comment has been flagged

But all the comments seem to be criticizing Paper-boy.
Can't say I admire the foul words, though.
They're still being sensible, right?
his comment has been flagged
his comment has been flagged
This comment has
Die, shithead
This comment has
This comment has been flag
Over 100 comments in the one day since it was re-posted ...
bullshit like
The comment section is pure pande-monium.
his comment has b
Die
This comment has
You really think so?
Huh?
All critical ...
"This comment has been flagged as spam."
... That label certainly stands out.
They're there because other users clicked the "Flag as spam" button.
his comment has
his comment has
This comment has
Looking closely at the com-ments,
Oh...
Yeah, you're right.
a whole lot of them are marked as spam, right?
This comment has been

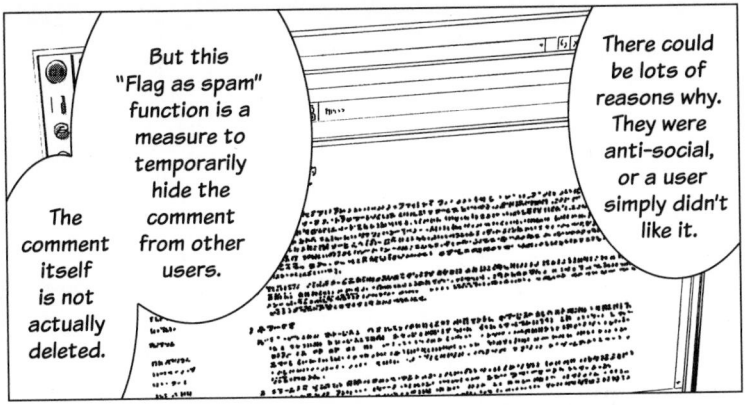
The comment itself is not actually deleted.
But this "Flag as spam" function is a measure to temporarily hide the comment from other users.
There could be lots of reasons why. They were anti-social, or a user simply didn't like it.

SHOW
KLIK

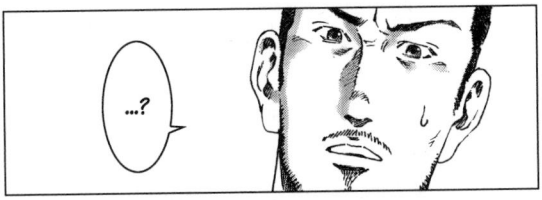
...?

If you click here,
it'll display the hidden comments.

FL
ASH
Go for it, Paperboy! I'm cheering you on, man!

I wish you'd come punish some people at my school, dude. Some of the teachers are pieces of shit.

Hide

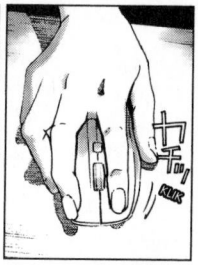

This newspaper guy is awesome! lol

watching ur video makes me feel brand new

That cockroach thing cracked me up! rofl

This comment has been flagged as spam.

Show

This comment has been flagg

got your back

Do it!

You're a her

Paperboy

I got you

Off the chain

at it's hilarious!

This comment has been flagged

This comment has been flagged a

This comment has been fl

omment has been flagged as sp

nment has b

d as sp

ment has

d as s

ent has b

ged as s

nment has been flagged as s

ment has been flagged as

nt has been flagged as

ed as

THESE PEOPLE ...

WHAT THE...

Even so, 280 people have clicked "Like."
95, 224
280 people
Dislikes 1,152 people
Right now the "Dislikes" have an overwhelming majority...
Just by looking at the user evaluation graph, you can see that he has an established support base.
280 people out of 1432...
That's 20%.
They'll take anything, so long as it's amusing.
That's what these people are like.
They just want to cause an uproar.
They're the walking personification of mob mentality.
They don't care a whit about justice or the law.
Even the accuracy of the information is not relevant.

But even a group like this can get out of control when their numbers swell.
We have to crush them, and soon.
Lt. Yoshino!
Phone call from the Cyber Force!
When I find the users reposting the videos for a lark,
HEH HEH
That'll just cause
I'll lock up a few as a lesson to the rest!
them to flame you.
Paperboy has posted a new video.
We're currently tracing the IP.

Like I already told you,
I don't do this for my own benefit.
So who do I do it for?
I do it for you.
The traitorous mass media is rotten to the core.
They've long since abandoned functioning like media should.
No one is hearing your voices.
So your voices can be heard.
I'm here to gather those voices and thrust them out into the open.
Oh!

Paperboy is back!
This guy's videos are so hilarious!
Nah, he's just some jerkwad.
It's probably that attention whore ____.
Who is that?
Is that the guy who was on the 2chan blog?
Huh? Who's he? Some celebrity?
I first saw him on Nico Nico.
It's heeeeere!
This is no time to be eating bamb
Has the new Paperboy vid come?
I heard he might do a live-stream.
He made a separate account on the streaming site.
Crap! Better take today off work!
DUTY FREE
TAKARATA

愛
UNI QLO
"PAPER-BOY"?
Spread the Word!
P oy Just dropped!! http;/ /byG
1,280 Retweets
Nice! It's here!
Retweet, retweet! ♪
It's frozen ...
Ooh! It's loaded !
The hell are ya doing?
Do your damn job, pigs!
Very slow con-nection today...
What's he gonna do this time...

Here's my warning for tomorrow.
facebook
Masayoshi Ikehata
+1 Add Friend
Masa-yoshi Ikehata.
The next target is an employee at a certain internet service firm in Tokyo.
NetWired
株式会社ネットワイヤード
大学
仙台駅南大学 法学部
he posted the following "liveblog" on a certain social networking site.
A few days ago, while conducting a hiring interview at his com-pany

32-year-old tech school grad's here for an interview... What to do with this geezer? lol
17:32
D-Dude's got balls!
17:35
Better go back to tech school myself!
17:35
Interviewing a guy that's older than me! lmfao! Should I liveblog this? lol
17:40
Bwahaha!! Do it!!!
17:41
"I went to [REDACTED] technical college. My name's [REDACTED] Shinyy-y-yya."
17:45
Mushmouth. Can't hear a fucking word he's saying! lolz
17:45
What a loser! haha
17:46
Ahahaha!! Oh shit! I nearly laughed out loud in the office!
17:48

This applicant had come to take the company's employment exam,
and he exposed him to public ridicule.
A 32-year-old man is there for a job interview,
and they find the situation so hilarious they nearly burst out laughing.
On the resume which the applicant submitted
there was apparently a blank period of several years.
Was he drifting?
Was he working part-time, or was he a NEET?
We don't know, but perhaps,
due to circumstances, he temporarily lost his footing and was derailed from society's tracks.

Yet even so, he tried to reintegrate into society by starting to hunt for a job.
Here is a man trying earnestly to do his level best.
Who has the right to turn him into a laughing-stock?
MASA-YOSHI IKEHATA.
I HEREBY SENTENCE THIS PIECE OF SHIT.
I WILL BEAT YOU INTO PULP.
1950円

I've got your back!
I'll spread this every-where!
klak klak
has been flagged as
Bwa ha ha !
Yeah, man! Go for it, yo!
Lame !
This is wild!
"Sen-tence"? The fuck?
So slow ...
KLIN
KTAN
...
...
This guy's a riot!
Hah !
KLIK
Flag as spam! Flag as spam !
Shit! I can't keep up!

KLIK
Requesting urgent deployment of officers from jurisdiction!
Ichikawa, have the Cyber Force on standby!
KLAK
We need personal protection for Masayoshi Ikehata and a security zone at key points in the environs of his house!
KLIK
KLAK
Continue the IP analysis!
DRIVE SLOWLY
Boss, the analysis is complete.
That was fast!
The location is W City, Saitama Prefecture. The W branch Pit Boy.
Got it. Ichikawa, head on over there.
Roger.
Is it from another Pit Boy location?
Yup.
Only the Paperboy likely isn't there, or hasn't even set foot inside.
It's probably a fool's errand, but it has to be checked out anyway.

We're heading to Masayoshi Ikehata's 2nd home. Street, N Block, O Ward. He'll definitely turn up there!
VROOMM
ブオオオオオ
Roger!

No breaking news interruption even at a time like this...
Bwa ha ha ha
Now, hang on a sec!
リフマップ

...

SNS. Aggregator blogs...
Your-tube.
Twitter.

I guess the era where TV as the stage for criminals with a flair for theatrics is over.

You mean TV's "jumped the shark"?
Heh heh.

May 22, 23:55
O WARD, TOKYO

ドガッ
WHUMP
Now to search for a wireless access point...
Good ...
This'll do.
TAR
_PORT_32T

Mmf ?!
Mnnn!!
Nnngg!!
I can crack a WEP key in 1 minute.
Just sit tight.

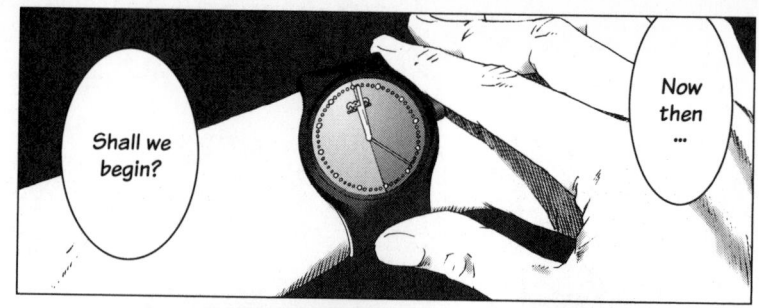
Now then ...
Shall we begin?

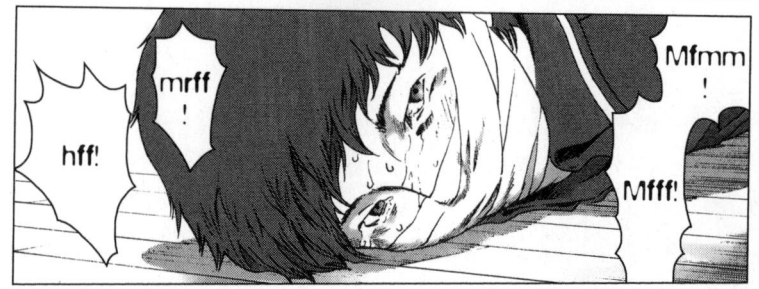
Mfmm !
Mfff!
mrff !
hff!

Hup !

File
004

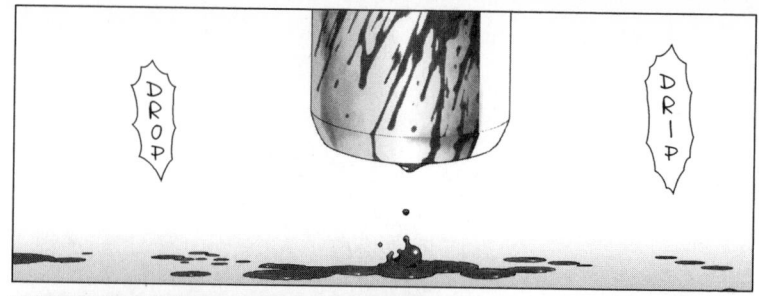

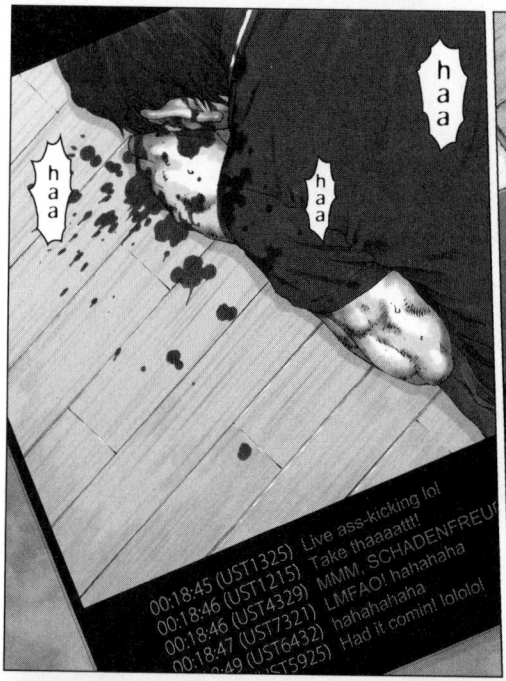

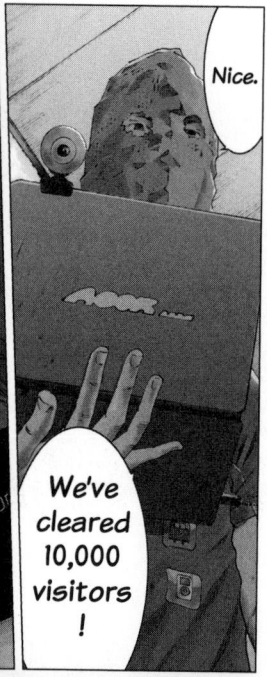

00:19:24 (UST9827) lolololololol
00:19:24 (UST9827) Had it comin! haha
00:19:25 (UST5678) Stop! Ikehata's down to zero life!
00:19:27 (UST6100) when r the cops gonna show up?!
00:19:30 (UST1533) get off your asses, cops! lol

Entry Team.
Proceed as soon as you're prepped.
May 23, 01:25
O WARD, TOKYO

You idiots! The perp's spreading a video of the beating to the whole damn world!
I want him stopped ASAP! Do you read me ?!
C-Copy that!
POL ICE

Huh ?
We're storming in already ?
Hey, hey! Without even a situ-ational analysis ?

Here we go!
Three, two—

SKREECH

What do you mean?
...It's empty ?

The volume is set quite high, probably
so the audio of the broadcast can be heard outside.

It's totally vacant.
Just a single computer displaying a live broadcast trans-mission.

There's definitely no furniture in the room in the streaming video.
SONY
He planned every little thing.

Probably not too far from here.
He must have prepared a room beforehand somewhere else in order to carry out his "sentence."

I'm emailing you the relay point.
Lieutenant Yoshino.
The perp is transmitting to the web via a WiFi connection.
RIRIRIRING

...
OK.
Except that's far too broad a range to set up a dragnet.
We can't pinpoint it with GPS-level precision,
but we can estimate that the perp is transmitting the video from within a 100-meter radius of this spot.
Or is he the "average-build man" who always posts the videos?
Is he the "chubby man" who abducted Shuji Seki ?
Is he a "tall, thin man" like the arsonist at Ishikawa?
In the streaming video
the perp took every caution to shoot it from an angle where we couldn't see his body.
Right now, we can't even be sure of that...
Or can that all be dismissed as eyewitness bias?

PHWEEET
Uhh ...
Let me confirm that again.
Suspect's profile ...

Age is late teens to 20's, or 30's.
Or possibly 40's.
Height is at least 5'5" or about 5'7".
Or around 5'11".
Body type is thin, medium-build, or plump.
Is that all? Please confirm.

So basically we're to question every single man that happens to walk by?
That is nuts.

Phew
KACHAK

That's just my luck.
The only incident I had to handle today was a report of a stolen bike from a pizza joint.
And just when I think I'll have a day that ends in peace for once, we get this.
Ha ha!
Don't get so bent outta shape over it.

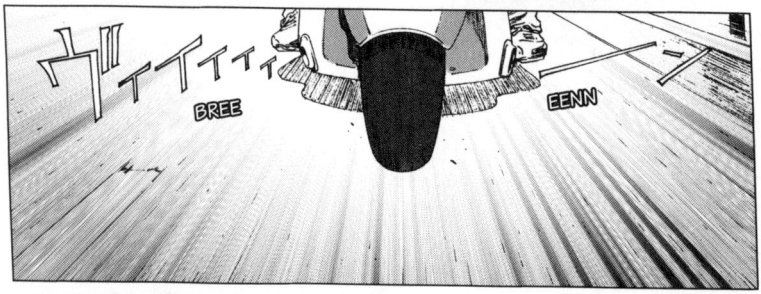
BREE
EENN

BREENN
...

VRUMM

If I was him I'd lose my shit, for real.
Bad form to waylay someone making a delivery.
... Hmm. Well.
PIZZA-U
PIZZA
HONDA
SKREE

An empty rental apartment ...
Ikehata was saved from the brink of death but he's covered in bruises, with 12 fractures.
He's also in deep psycho-logical shock.
No inter-viewing him for a while, it seems.
But how did the perpetrator get a key to the place?
It seems nobody has leased this apartment yet.
Welcome, new resident of # 201
He pro-bab-ly
got it from here.

Look. Marks from someone forcibly prying it open.
Ah ...
The meter box...?
There's a spare in here?
When you've got a vacancy up for lease like this place,
they often leave a key in the meter box or mailbox.

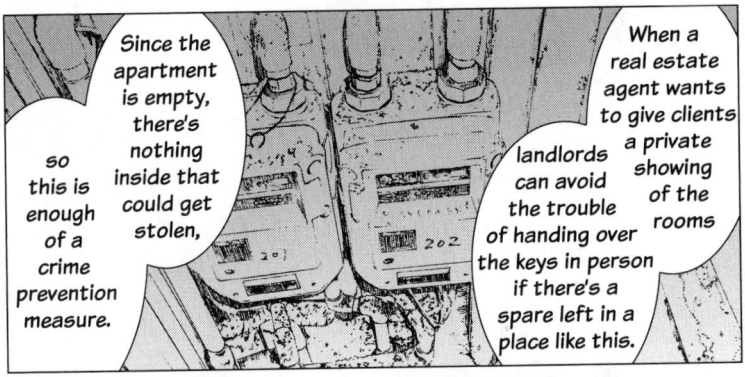
Since the apartment is empty, there's nothing inside that could get stolen,
so this is enough of a crime prevention measure.
When a real estate agent wants to give clients a private showing of the rooms
landlords can avoid the trouble of handing over the keys in person if there's a spare left in a place like this.

So this was all pre-meditated ?

An empty apart-ment like this one
would be the perfect temporary space for committing a crime.

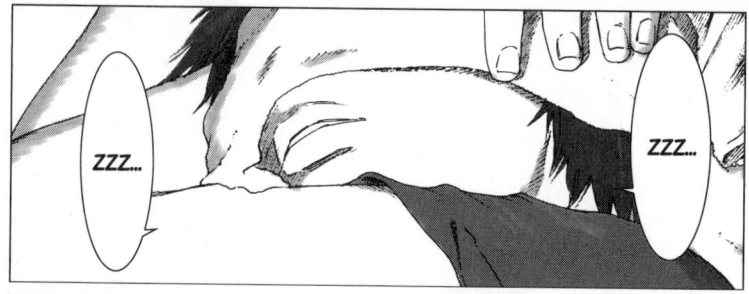
ZZZ...
ZZZ...

ZZZ...
ZZZ...

KLAK KLAK KLAK KLAK

OKUDA! HAVE YOU FINISHED MODULE 8 YET?!
YES! IT'LL BE READY IN 3 MIN-UTES!
KLAK KITY KLAK KITY KLAK
...
Okuda, you're en-thused lately.
Nab a girl-friend?
Ha ha! I'll have been here 3 years next month.
I'll be made a full-time employee.
Oh. That's right. You're on contract, yeah?
Well, con-grats.
Thanks.

Wha... Please, boss! Give me a break!
It's what I've been working towards this whole time!
Be-come a full-time employ-ee?
I don't remember us having a system like that!
Uh... well, other than JAVA ...
I looked at a bit of PHP and C++...
Hmm. Well, that may be, but...
Okuda, What did you learn in school other than JAVA?
Hmf.
C... just the basics.
That was mostly self-taught.
What about C?

I see lots of you types lately.
Kids who get a bit of JAVA under their belt
and then they're like, "I'm a programmer!"
Yeah, man.
Right.
The entry point for kids these days is object-oriented programming.
That shit's fuckin' useless.
Huh ...?
What the...
Is this turning into an attack on me ...?

Makes it real hard to look at. Could you stop that?
You've a habit of putting in line breaks in weird places.
Another thing, Okuda.
Yes ?
Yeah. Could you?
Should I fix all the work I've done already, too?
Oh...! Sorry. I'll be more care-ful.
Today ?
What ...
Fix it today.
Also, on this pro-ject,
the client's changed the specs.
That could be pretty tough...
Well, but...

Yes, sir.
Understood.
Do it.
KLATTER
Uh... umm.
President Horii.
It's your job.
About formatting the code and that stuff...
If possible, could you please tell me sooner, so...
Well...
It would help me get things done on time.

A damn temp's finding fault with my work.
Well that's some shit. What'll I do?
Huh?
What?
You saying I give bad direction?
N-No, sir!
That's not what I...
Not at all!
GET IT?!
YOU'RE NOT A FUCKING BABY!!
Listen here! If there's something you don't understand, then ask!!

Sorry ...
I'm very sorry, sir...
HUSSHH...

KLAKKLAK
klak klak
haa
klakkak
haa

Un ...
!
... Sorry.
You can stop.
Can I ask you to go clean or something ?

It's my fault for giving you too much work.
... No.
I'm to blame.
KDAK
I- I'm sorry !
I just... drifted off for a second.
I apologize ...
Wha ?
Real-ly?
SQUIK
SQUIK
TWIST

The deadline's actually next week, isn't it.
And that project.
HOLY SHIT, YOU'RE SCARY !
If he fucks it up, what happens to the company's cred, huh?
Aaagh! You're a mon-ster!
Of course it is.
I'm not gonna give some pipsqueak temp a job with a tight deadline!
HA HA HA
HA HA HA
Well... Either way, I hope he quits, and soon.

'cause he's totally useless.
BIP
...

ニッコリ生放送
NICCORI LIVE
It's heeeeeeeerrrre!!
Nice work!
Paperboy's here!!!
Nice nabbin this slot!
It's heeeeeeerre!
Good job!
not sold out
Good goin'!
nabbed a spot
Live nico this time? lol
Paperboy's here!
COMMENTS
COMMENTS
COMMENTS
NICCORI LIVE
No warning yet today?
What about the warning?
I took this broadcast slot because there's something I want to tell you.
There will be no warning today.
1. YES 42.5%
2. 57.5%
...I see.
Quite a number of you.
Any of you out there right now contract workers?
Part-timers? Short-term factory workers?
Perhaps I should say "atypical employment."

Live on Niccori ?!
Lieutenant Yoshino!
The Paperboy is broadcasting live on Niccori!
It's not the usual warning video post, is it.
Well ...
He's saying there's something he wants to say.
Without self-respect, a person cannot survive.
If they lose that, they can pretend they're still alive
but that's not a condition which I can call "living."

The things I hate most in this world
are those which robbed you of the self-respect you once had.
They are hidden in places throughout society.
...
NSURANCE PREMIUM
TURES LEASE CHARGE
E PROCESSING FEE
NSUMPTION TAX
TOTAL
Confusing line items on your payslip.
Arrogant cops who stop and question you.
The conversation in the office kitchen that you overhear.
The stare of someone who brushes past you on the street.

Yes ...
I get it.
but that pent-up resentment you feel right now?
I cannot improve the quality of your lives
I can relieve you of that, just a little.
From now on
if someone wounds your pride without cause, tell me about it.

I WILL KILL THEM.
So don't stash any of it away.

刺殺予告か
者、事件前交番に
I SWEAR I WILL.

onymous
n a woman, but I think h
as a point.

nonymous
Got fuckall to do with wom
n lol

691. Anonymous
Yeah there's jerks like
this at my office. Only the
ones who're totally fuckin
useless have an overblo
sense of pride.

692. Anonymous
Feels like I've been waiti
forever to hear someone
say this. I've been a part
net lynchings trying to ta
my mind off things, but i
just empty and pathetic.
so totally pathetic you ca

693. Anonymous
@692 Fuck off.

694. Anonymous
@692 Please stop!

398 Anonymous@2011/5/23 05:23
MPD notification!

399 Anonymous@2011/5/23 05:23
Oh so NOW they're fast

400 Anonymous@2011/5/23 05:23
fuckin pigs
Don't you have more important

YOU CAN'T SUPPRESS FREE SPEECH

This guy's a real pain in the ass.
Feels like the more we try to strike at him, the more enemies we make.
Lieu-tenant Yoshi-no.
Please look at this.
Ah...

What's wrong ?
I can't believe this is happening.
No way ...

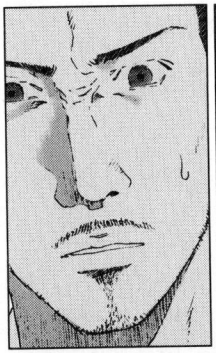

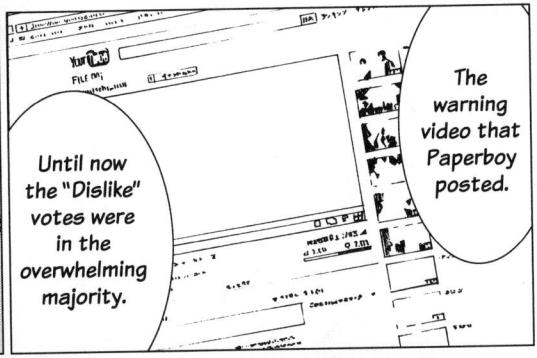
Until now the "Dislike" votes were in the overwhelming majority.
The warning video that Paperboy posted.

the approving votes have surpassed the disapproving ones!
68,574 views
2,683
But now

PROPHECY

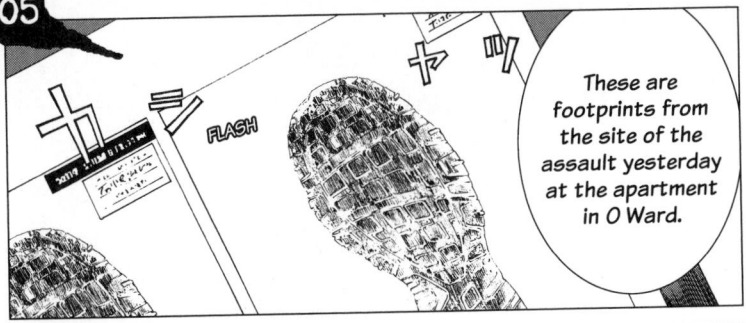
FLASH
These are footprints from the site of the assault yesterday at the apartment in O Ward.

Both are men's size 8 1/2.
Both are of the same make.
But there's one distinct difference:

They match those found
at the site of the food processor arson in Ishikawa Prefecture on May 21.
FORENSICS

There is a large amount of weight on the heel of the Ishikawa print.
That section alone has a darker shading than the rest.
What does this mean?

One possibility is that there are two people of different height and weight
wore the same size shoes from the same brand in order to pose as a single person.

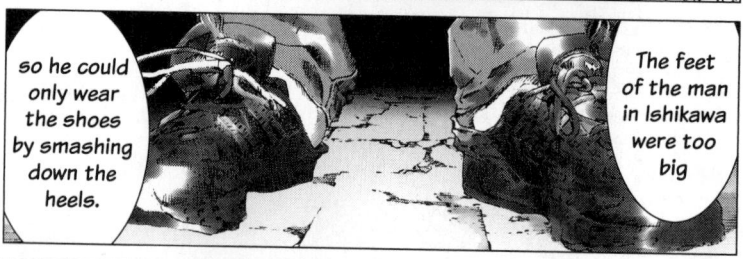
The feet of the man in Ishikawa were too big
so he could only wear the shoes by smashing down the heels.

We can't really say any more than that...
But we can assume it's highly probable
that a coconspirator is involved in this series of crimes.

Shoes that didn't fit...
What for?
Senior Superintendent
KOTARO TAKAGI

File
005

Yoshino,
I'd like to hear your opinion.

Your predictions tend to be right.
I'll ask point-blank:
Just what is it that they want?

I still don't know their true goals,
but their primary aim
is to fashion a shared character, I believe.

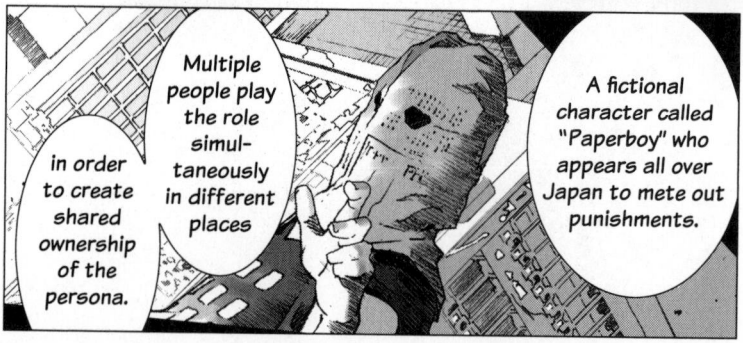
A fictional character called "Paperboy" who appears all over Japan to mete out punishments.
Multiple people play the role simultaneously in different places
in order to create shared ownership of the persona.

At first, I thought this string of crimes could be explained by the "smart mob" concept.
A shared character.
The same clothes even the same shoes, eh?

The concept is a totally new manifestation of group power that's impossible with traditional media.
People with highly-developed information devices meeting and then acting in concert online.
What's a smart mob?

I thought this was basically the scenario.
then a kind of group mentality comes into play, and it becomes impossible to curb.
Eventually, people emerge who begin actually carrying out crimes,
They half-jokingly chat about planning crimes without ever knowing each other's names or faces.
Users meet each other on anonymous message boards online.

Yes.
When I saw yesterday's live broadcast, I changed my mind.
Hmm... I see.
I can see how such a thing would be possible nowadays.
But now you think differently?
The man in front of the webcam stating he won't forgive those in our society who rob others of their self-respect...
I think he's probably the ringleader.
I felt a powerful strength of purpose in his eyes.
But what could have given him such resolve...?

Excuse me.
Lieutenant Yoshino.
We have a report from the Cyber Force.

They finally worked out the posting location of FILE001.
The springboard was the net café in A City, Kanagawa Prefecture ...
but the original source of the transmission was here.

Inside ...
Tokyo ?

May 23, 14:00
M TOWN, TOKYO
So, I take it you rigorously check IDs?
fssh
...I see.
24h PITBOY
I applied by the law!
Yes, of course!
"Abide," you mean.
KAPOP

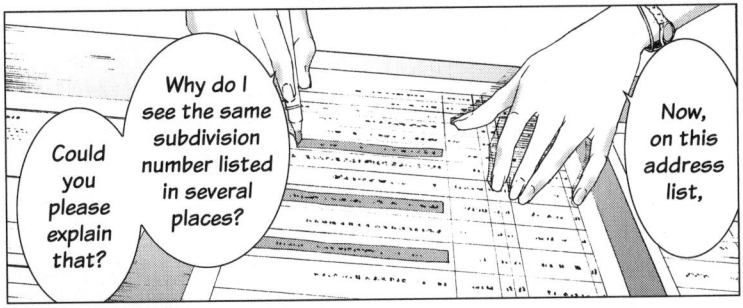
Now, on this address list,
Why do I see the same subdivision number listed in several places?
Could you please explain that?

Ah... ha...
No... well, y'see...
How to put it... ha ha ...

These unnaturally redundant addresses are all
this shop's address, aren't they?

You're aware of the Metropolitan ordinance regarding net café businesses enacted July 2010, are you not?
Y...
Yes.
But, it's... well...

I'd put in this address in their place, so...
So I mean, I feel like maybe I did that or maybe I didn't but...
And well, some of those older customers didn't have any ID...
It's just tempo-rary...
Yes, a temp mea-sure.
But the thing is
to bother those who were customers before the ordinance was enacted to produce ID yet again... that's a little...

Now then, we'll go get a search warrant from court
and we'll conduct an official investigation with full legal force.
A... A war-rant ?!

STRIKE-OUT!
Wha aaa aaa ....!

Like an in-vestiga-... tion... sorta ?
Th- That's ...

An actual criminal investigation.
スチャ
SLIDE
Not...
"sorta."

All right, then instead, will you let us borrow your customer list
and security camera footage for our investigation?
Wait, plee eee eee ase!
NO NO NO NO NO NO!
It could potentially result in an immediate suspension of business, I hope you understand.

PLEASE, TAKE ANYTHING YOU NEED!
OH, WITH PLEASURE!

WHURR
DINNG

That the perp was in Kanagawa or Saitama.
I-I...
You were so sure of yourself.
I was only talking about poten-tialities.

So, Ichi-kawa.
Your hunch was off.
What are you talking about ?

5F
That's inconse-quential.
Okamoto.

What's important is that our criminal anticipated beforehand that we'd think
that he was likely to avoid using any Tokyo branches.
This man is able to guess what the police will assume
and has the wits and technical skills to outfox us.
4F
5F·6F
If he hadn't, then going to the trouble to reach across another prefecture
to login remotely would be inexpli-cable.
Oh... right.
For sure.
This isn't something an incompetent person could do.
We'd best realize we're dealing with a very crafty individual.

We may be able to take advantage of that.
However, the criminal does not yet know that we know.
Not a night owl?
Oh... no.
But you're still so young.
I just, erm...
For now, let's book the monitor room at the local precinct and check the videos.
Might take us all night.
A-All night ...?
...
A very crafty individual, huh...
to get the boss to admit he's smart ...
To think someone was able

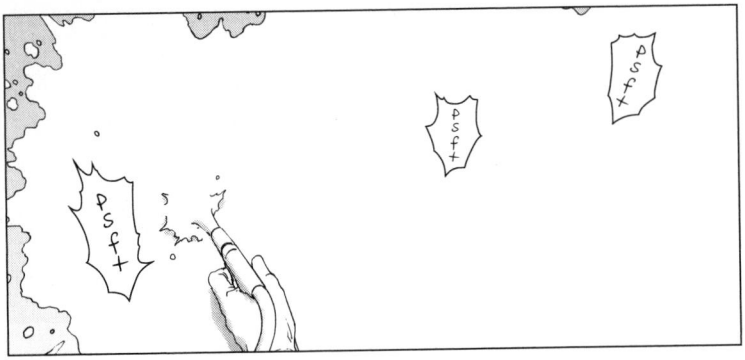
PSFT
PSFT
PSFT

SQUEEEEK
UH
UHN

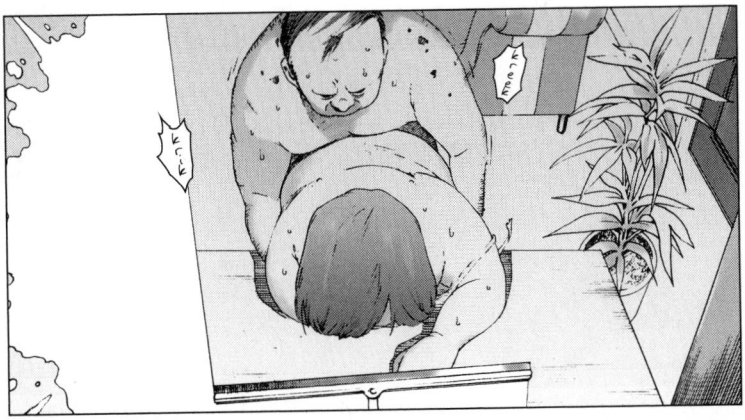
EEEEE
EEEEE

HAA
HAAA
ゴクッ
Ahn!
sagg
sagg

AH!
Apf!
AAH!
KREAK
HAA
KREAK
HAA

May 23, 15:30
METROPOLITAN POLICE DEPARTMENT,
M TOWN PRECINCT STATION

COMPUTER
ROOM
PC ROOM
In Use
Metro
Police Dept 3 p.m.
Yoshino

Ah...

こんーと
こんーと
...

TWIST
キュルル

Boss, I've found something.
It's probably him.
That was fast.
Oh!
Let me zoom in a bit closer.
This video.
Look at the angle of the man's head.

But if this video is all we're going on,
Or he slept funny ?
couldn't we simply assume that it's a habit?
From the angle of his head
it certainly seems he's conscious of the security camera.
twice failed to pick up his change
yet still stubbornly kept his face angled down.
In that case, he ought to angle his whole body to face the register.
However, this man
...
One other thing.
SNAP
Here's a video taken from a different angle inside the café.

Ah...

So it's because he knew all about the positions of the cameras before-hand
that he's displaying this unnatural behavior.

Now it's down to the left...
I see.

Your vigilance has backfired,
Paper-boy.

NOMOTO CLEANING
I deeply apolo-gize, sir...
Yes... Yes, sir.
Of course ...
Believe me, I will tell him.
Yes ...
Yes, sir... I'm very sorry.
Is that so, sir?
Oku-daaa !!

'bout what ?
Is there anything you wanna tell me?

Oh, is that so.
Do not invade people's privacy, you fucking pervert !!
I just got a furious complaint from a tenant in the Shitaragi Building!

Really ?!
Wha ?!
THANKS TO YOU, THEY'VE CANCELLED OUR CONTRACT NEXT TERM!
DON'T "IS-THAT-SO" ME, DIPSHIT !

...
How you gonna fix this, huh?! I'm serious!!
The contract that my wife
bowed and scraped in order to secure for us!
Are we done now?
...I'm real sorry.
WHMM
WHY, YOU !!

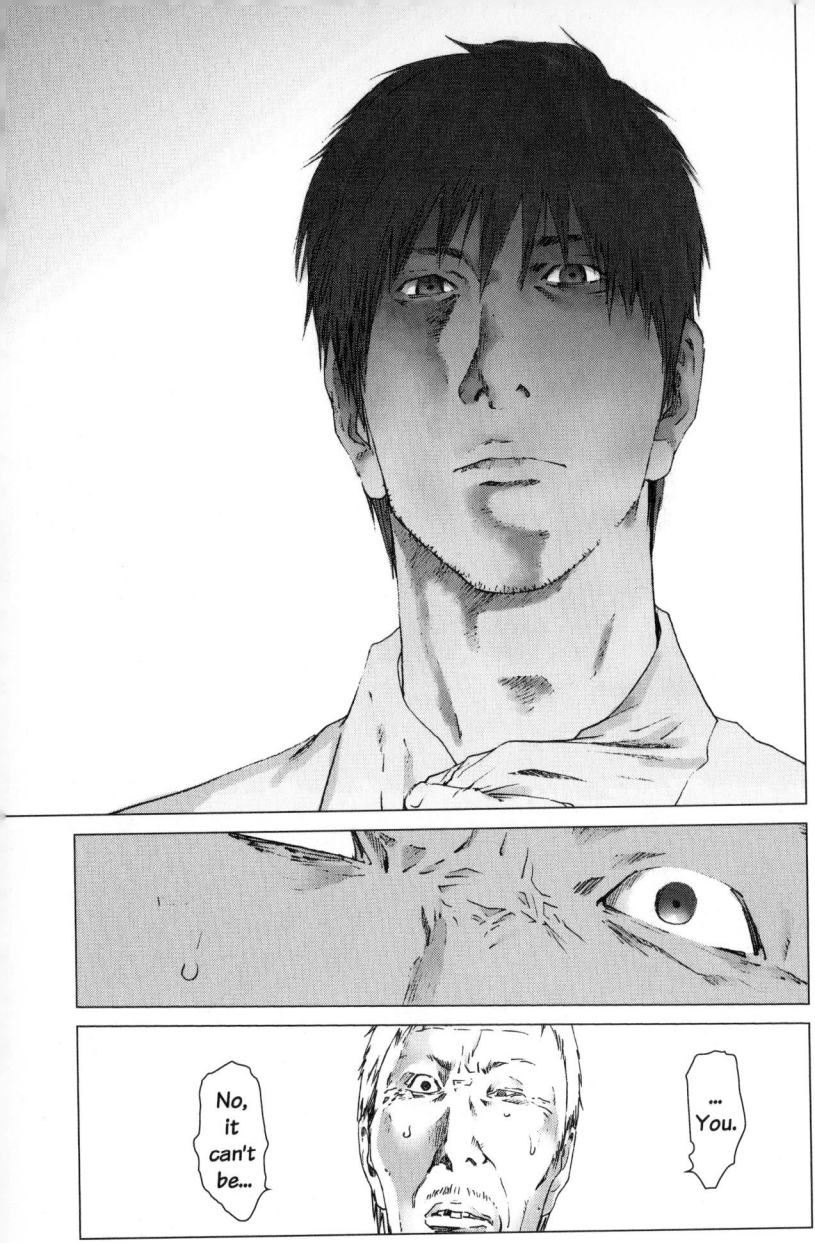
No, it can't be...
... You.

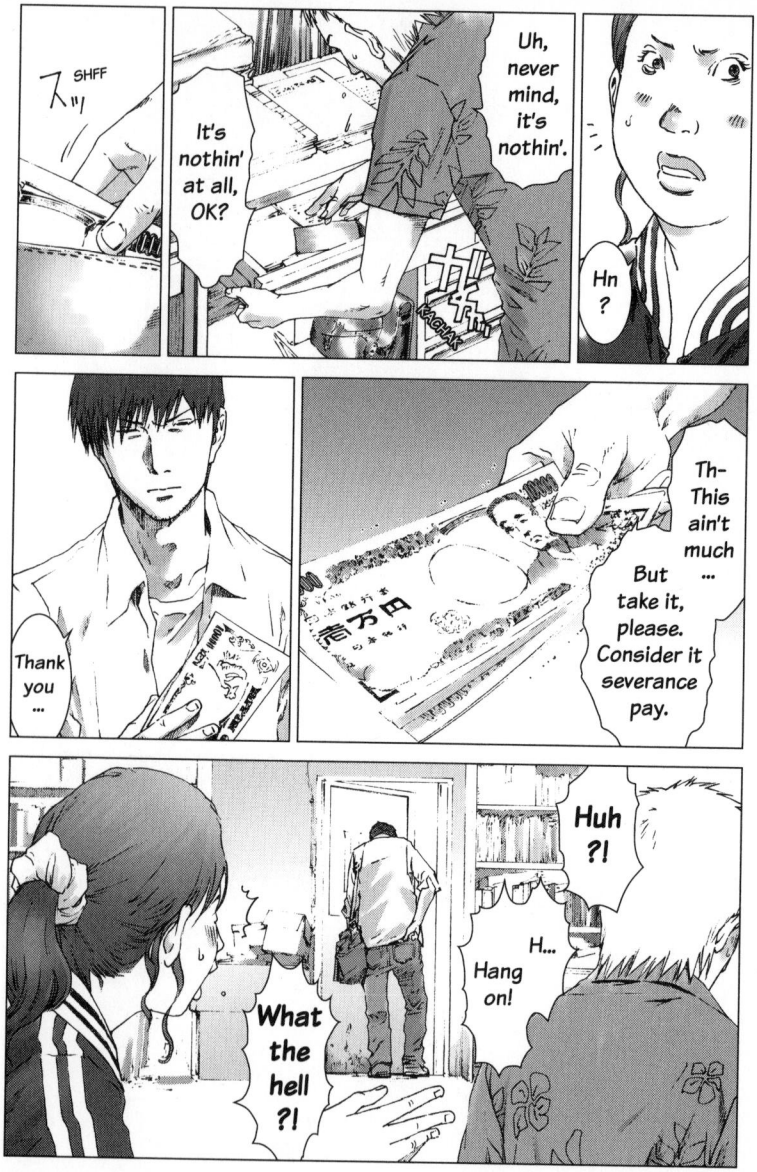
スッ SHFF
It's nothin' at all, OK?
Uh, never mind, it's nothin'.
ガチャ KACHAK
Hn ?
Thank you ...
Th- This ain't much ...
But take it, please. Consider it severance pay.
Huh ?!
H... Hang on!
What the hell ?!

Huh ?!
What were you gonna say before ?!
You're just gonna shut up and let him go ?!
I...
It's not like I can say it...

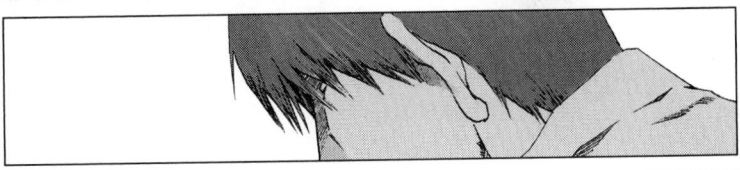

...no way...
"You've killed a man, haven't you?"
I can't say...

This is the usage log for the afternoon of May 18.
This was the person who used booth 8.
May 23, 16:45
PITBOY, M TOWN BRANCH, TOKYO
24H FITNESS

Nelsin Kato-Ricarte

Wait, a foreigner?
Ri-carte?
Nelsin Kato...
What the...

I wonder.
I think "Kato" is a name that's used in the West, too.
He could be of Japanese descent.
A parent could have had the Japanese surname "Kato."

But from what we saw in the video, he was clearly Asian, right?
Oh...
Yeah.
His speech was just like a typical Japanese person.

So he wouldn't have needed any ID to register at the time...
His membership card was issued on August 23, 2007,
before the ordinance was enforced.

Then we can consider the possibility that he completely cooked the name up.
But if so, why would he choose to use such a foreign-sounding name?
There could be some reason.
I'll make inquiries at the Immigration Bureau.
I'll get them to do a search prior to August 2007.
Please do that.
...

...
Nelsin Kato-Ricarte...
That's not your name either, is it,
Paperboy ?

PROPHECY

File
006

September 20, 2008
4:30 AM

September 20. Once more I've not a single yen to my name.
As always, I've come to the "day labor market" to wait for the "recruiter."
After I got fired from the software company, I started doing day labor.
No interview, resume or prior contact needed.
Just show up at the market and you're picked up as a hired hand.
You can tell who your "coworkers" are just by looking at them
but you never speak with each other.
ブロロロ

"Light work" really means "no technical skills required."
I guess this, too, is industry jargon.
It definitely does not mean "easy work."
Need 5 guys for light work.
Young fellas get priority.
Let that bro with the glasses on through.
That's it for today.
Hang on there.
Not you.
Some day it'll be me.
Even in this business, if you're too old, you get weeded out.

However, we later learned that on this occasion

those who had been weeded out were the lucky ones.

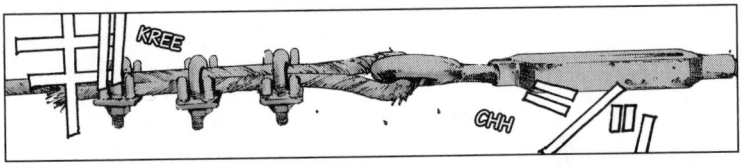

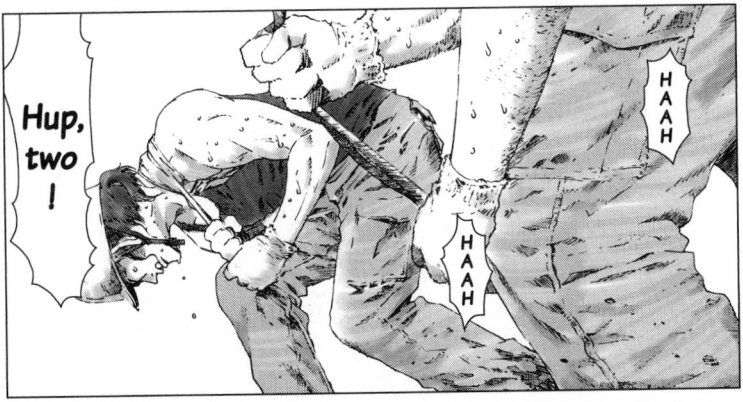

GRIKK
GREE
HFF
WHEW

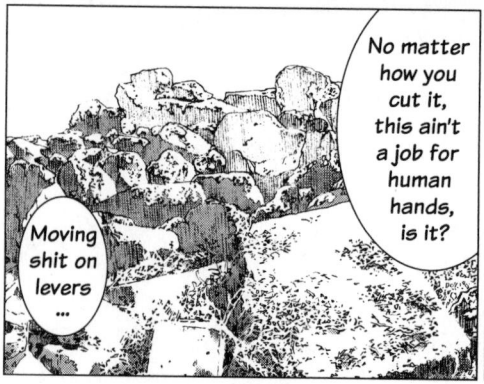
No matter how you cut it, this ain't a job for human hands, is it?
Moving shit on levers ...

Hey ...
It's the 21st century, ain't it?
Huh ?

Why the fuck're we relying on levers?!
This the stone age?
Haa!
This company's too stingy to pay for heavy machinery.
I'be blunt ...

Crude oil, eh.
Crude oil's price is surging.
Oil's getting stupidly expensive this year.
I heard an economist on TV say that
the amount of money in the world economy exceeded the amount of product.
And that exorbitant excess wealth was always seeking someplace to go
which sent prices into turmoil.
CRAKK
Aagh!

So some fat pigs could get even fatter.
HEY, YOU !
STOP HELPING HIM!
Let me tell you the rule around here.
Don't help anyone who collapses.

That alone was the reason years of our lives were being shaved off.
If he falls, let him.
That's his busi-ness.
I can replace him.
But if someone helps him, I lose the work of two men.
I won't stand for that.

The day-to-day work was harsh
but the atmosphere in the worker's lodge certainly wasn't bad.

It's written on your hat.
SOLTBA
HAW
FUKUOKA
Oh ...!

You're from Fukuoka, aren't ya, bro?
Hm? Yeah.
Was it my accent ?

HA HA
HA HA HA
Aw, man.
I just fuckin' love the Hawks.

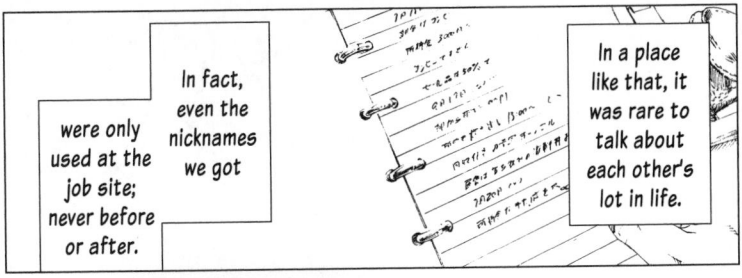
In a place like that, it was rare to talk about each other's lot in life.
In fact, even the nicknames we got
were only used at the job site; never before or after.

Word got out that I had worked in IT
so they just started calling me "Gates."
...Well, nicknames are never all that serious.

This guy was born in Osaka, so we called him "Kansai."
He'd come to Tokyo to try to make it as a musician, but apparently failed.
If you got him started on the corrupt nature of the Japanese music industry, he'd rant for hours.

HAWKS
FUKUOKA
"Tubby" from Fukuoka.
He was only 31, but having neglected his health he'd grown quite a belly.
He was obsessed with pachinko, and had given up the idea of inheriting his family's engineering firm.
He was fond of saying, "Man, the 4th gen machines sure were sweet."
"Nobita" from Miyagi.
A man of very few words.
After high school, it seems he lived as an unemployed shut-in for a while,
but when his father died of kidney failure, he made up his mind to start working.
He had a phobia of women and was obsessed with PC-based dating sims.

And this was "Slim," a Filipino of Japanese descent.
All of us lowering our guards with each other in that cesspit of a job site
was thanks to his innocent affability.

Slim had grown up in a slum named "Smokey Mountain,"
the absolute poorest area of the Philippines.

Just before his mother died of illness, she'd told him his father was Japanese.
So he desperately saved up enough money to come to Japan and search for him.

Once he got here he worked for a while as a janitor in a net café in Tokyo,
but the boss kept withholding his pay, so he ended up quitting.
Slim wasn't strong, so he wasn't cut out for physical labor,
but the number of places that will employ a foreigner without a work visa is limited.
And then the manager of the café fled one night and it went bankrupt.
He'd sure seemed to have had a rough life,
AH HA!
but strangely I never got a sense of sorrow from the guy.

What's up, Slim?
What is that thing?
HAWKS
FUKUOKA

I got five today!
Yay!
625C74

If you press this beepy button it shows numbers.
Don't really know, but...

Some kinda lottery machine ?
BIP
But if you get a whole bunch of numbers, that's lucky!
Letters, too.
HAWKS
FUKUOKA

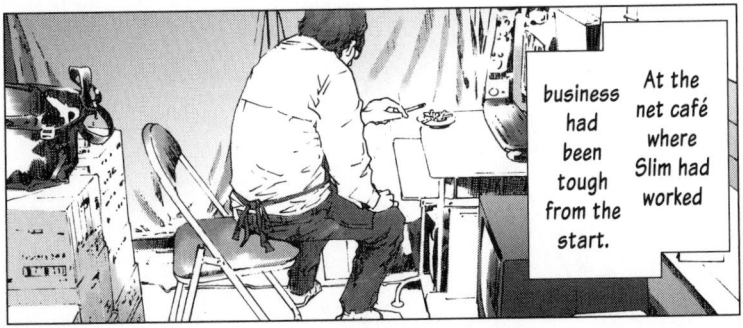
At the net café where Slim had worked
business had been tough from the start.

Some time after he'd quit,
unaware that the manager had run for it,
Slim went back to the café to try to collect his back pay.
The place was deserted,
but in the back of the office, he'd found this "lottery machine."
Slim.
Can I see that for a second ?
BEEP
BEEP
This might be...
some kind of security key.

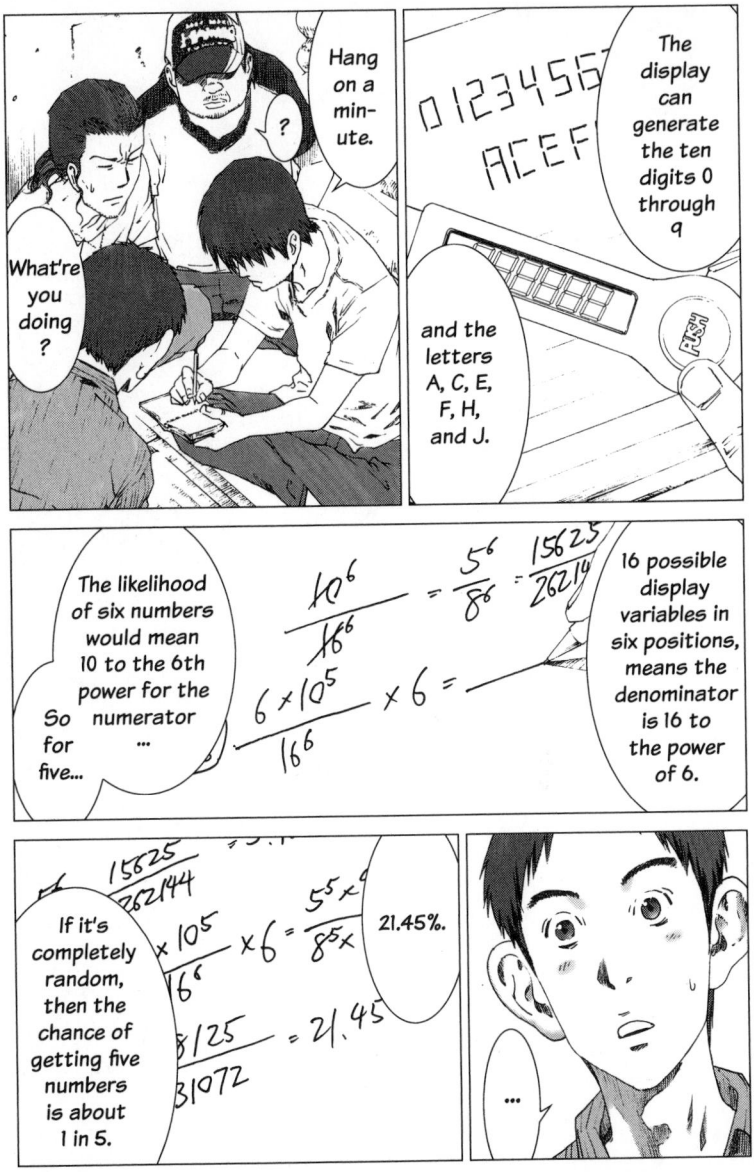
Hang on a minute.
?
What're you doing ?
The display can generate the ten digits 0 through 9
and the letters A, C, E, F, H, and J.
The likelihood of six numbers would mean 10 to the 6th power for the numerator ...
So for five...
16 possible display variables in six positions, means the denominator is 16 to the power of 6.
If it's completely random, then the chance of getting five numbers is about 1 in 5.
21.45%.
...

The chance of getting numbers in all six positions is 1 in 17.
The prob-ability's not too bad.
If you try it daily, you'll get it some day.
Whoa ...!
Then I should get it about once a week, right?
But I guess I'll almost never get all numbers, huh?
That's our IT man!
That's amazing !
You did that with no calcula-tor!
You're unreal, man.
HA HA HA
Y-Yeah, that's right ...
S-Sure ...
This is 11th grade math.
Every-body learns this, right?

You're a weird one.
You want this?
Sure, I guess ...
Hey... Say, Gates.
Can I have that paper ?
Huh ...?
Amazing ...!
It looks like a magic spell!

Gates! Teach me how to do math!
S-Sure ...
I wanna learn how to do this, too!

From that day on, I started teaching Slim in the evenings like a private tutor.

Slim had hardly any formal education, but he was a quick learner.
He mastered the four rules of arithmetic as soon as I'd taught him.

Your pay is 750 yen an hour, so how much do you get for 6 hours?
Umm ...
750 times 6, that's... 4500?
Yes.
There's a 5% income tax withheld, so
what's left is your share.

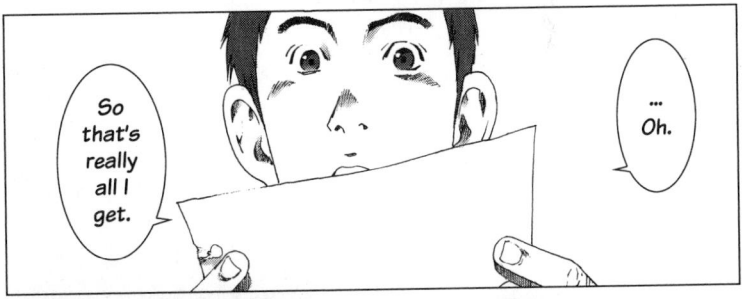
... Oh.
So that's really all I get.

Slim.
You're not dumb.
You just never had the chance to get an education.

Thank you, Gates.
I was fooled 'cause I'm so dumb.

BLAZE
C-Can't fuckin' believe this...
Hot as hell in late September.
Heard it's gonna be over 85°F.
HAAA
HAA
Aah!
SLIM!

... Itchy ?

But I'm just
so itchy... all over...

Can't you eat any more ?
Don't push your-self.
No ...
Sorry, Gates.

Slim. Could I...
have a look at your back?

Yeah ...
Itchy.
'cause I haven't had a bath...

Your kidneys are failing.
Slim, you ...
Y-Yeah. It hurts, it hurts.
Ow!
Does it hurt here?
Kidney failure?
Wha...?
He looked like his face was made from clay
and he got bloated and itchy all over.
My dad died from bad kidneys, too.
Anything that might have overburdened your body?
Slim... do you have any ideas?
Just like you are now.

To come to Japan ...
I needed... lots of money ...
No-bita ...
I'm sor-ry.
I... never told you.
So...
I... sold one.
I sold
a kidney ...

...
actually do that shit?!
Do people
FUKUOKA
S...
Sold a kidney ...?
But I've been ...
... sick ever since.
Anemic ...
Back... pain.
Faint ...
But I heard that even if you give up one kidney for a transplant, it doesn't affect your health.
That's if it's done in a proper hospital.
Gates.
Guess I really am dumb.
I wanted to come to Japan.
Ruined my health ...
I sold my kidney.

He needs to be on dialysis in a hospital.
We can't just let him lie in a place like this.
Slim...
We're out of range here.
But how?
A hos-pital ...?
Go get the foreman.

3 4
3 4

File 007

So he's dead.
... Oh.

It'll be just you four on the job 'til then.
Well, happens all the time.
I'll fill the vacancy tomor-row.
TOSS
Use this.
THW
UNK

Hurry up and bury him,
'fore he rots.

DAB
フキ
DAB
フキ
SOLT BANK
HAWKS
FUKUOKA
What's wrong ?
Don't just stand there, get movin—

CHO
KK

The fuck is wrong with you ?!!

KR
ASH
You
...

DON'T YOU FUCKIN' STOP ME!
CATCH
I'm not stop-ping you.
Huh ?

I'm not stop-ping you.
Let me have it.

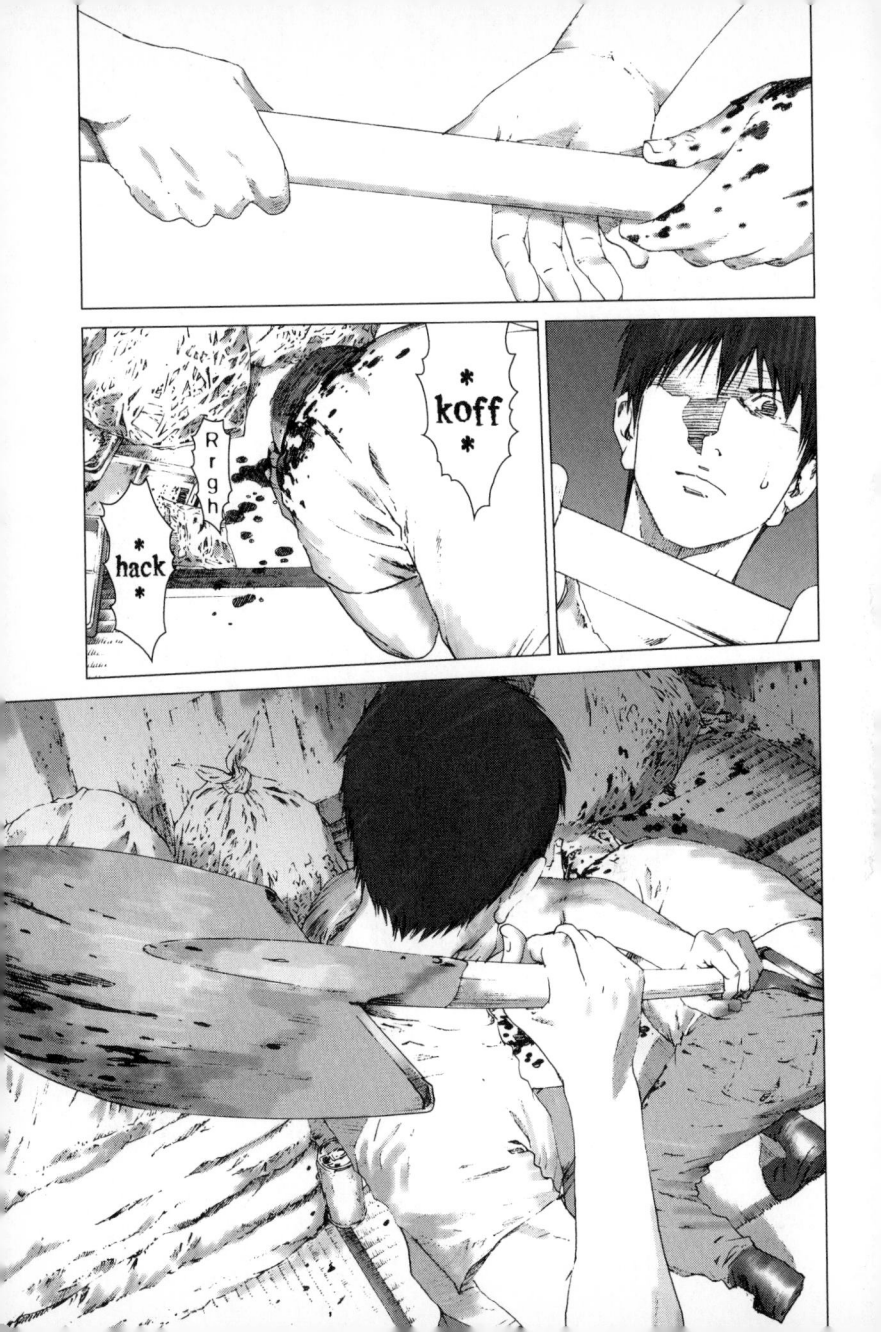
koff
Rrgh
hack

ZM
ASH

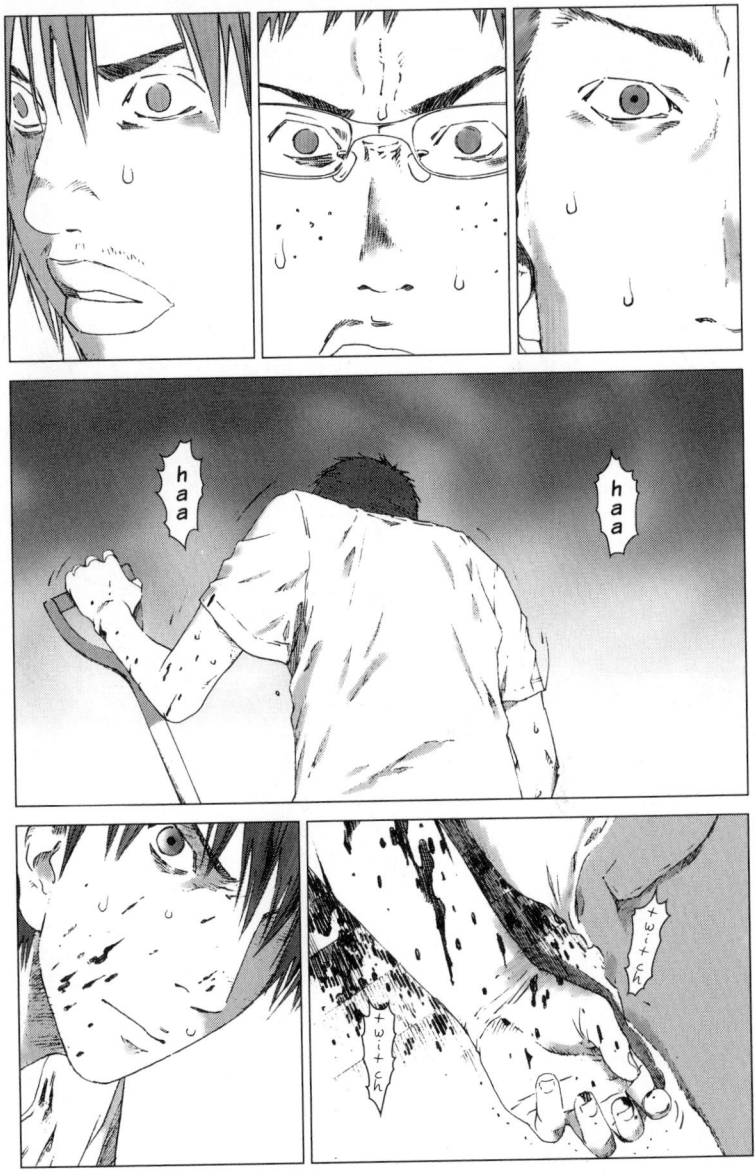
haa
haa
ちゃっ
ちゃっ

haa
haa

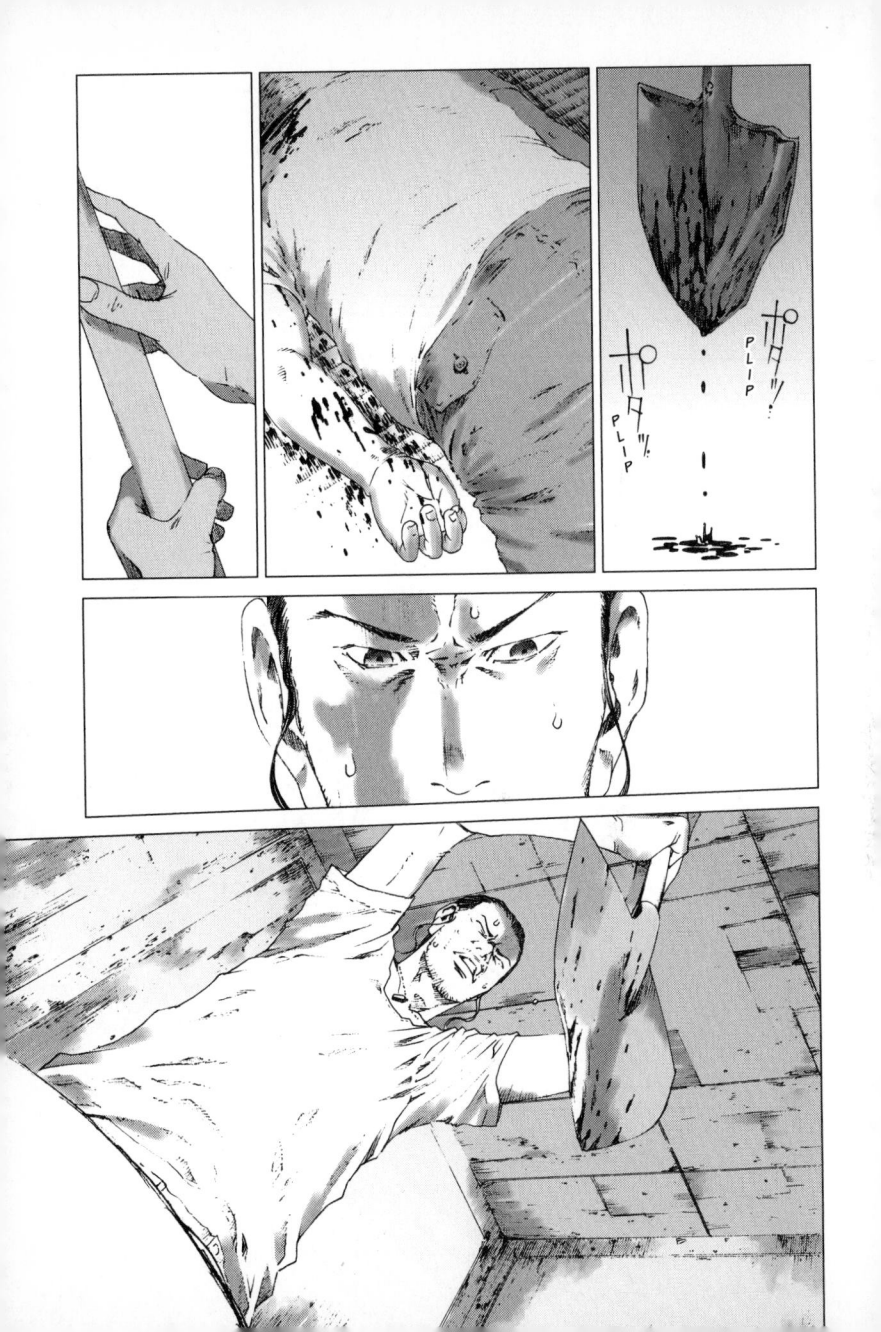
ポタッ!!
PLIP
ポタッ!!
PLIP

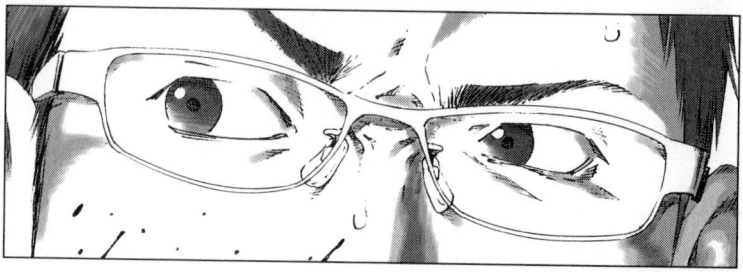

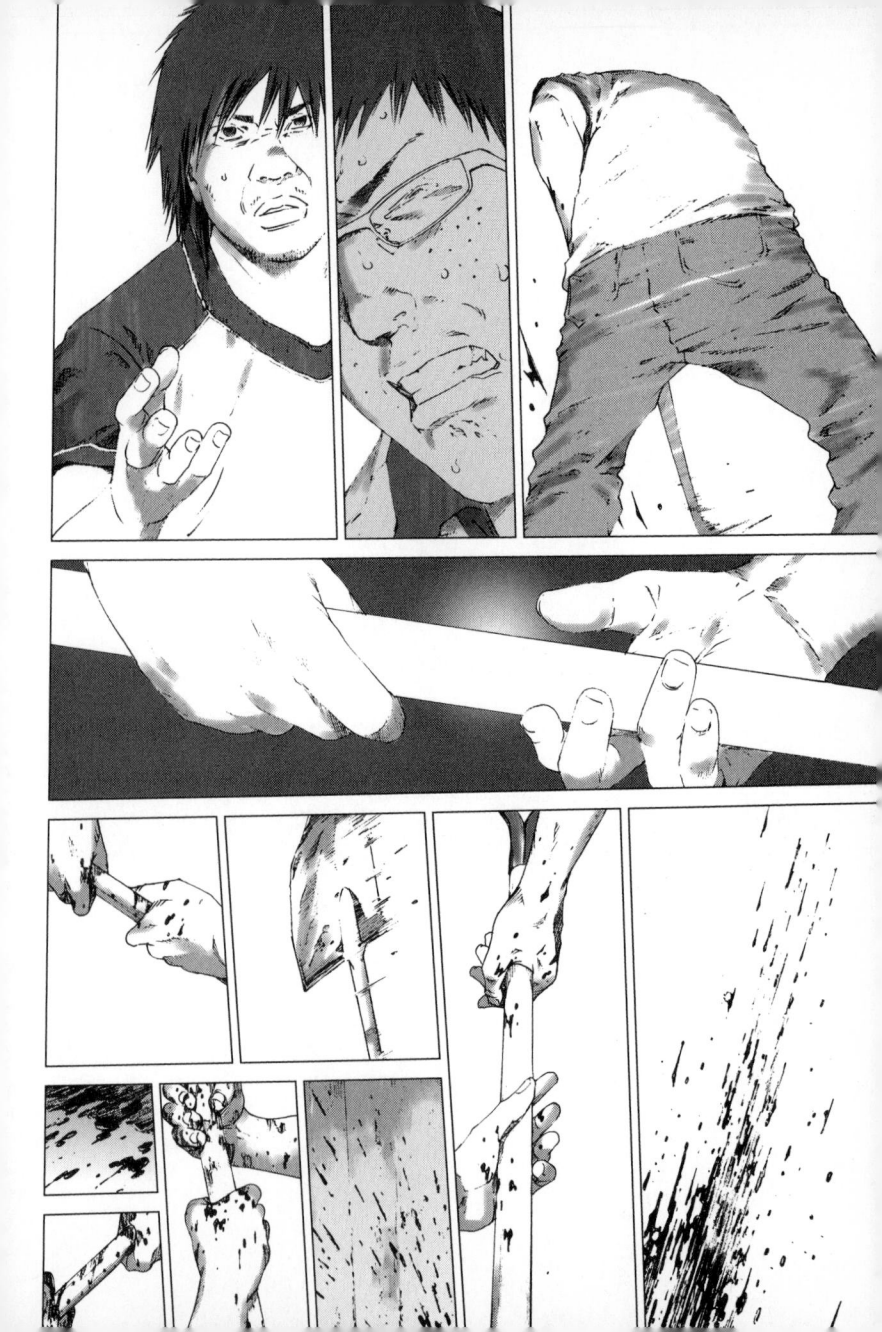

ROO
ARR

Arson, murder. Abandonment of a corpse.
We'll get life in jail when we go back to the city.
Forget about it.
If you hadn't done it, I would have.
... Sorry
I dragged you guys into this.
My life was in checkmate ever since I got hooked on pachinko anyways.
Gave up on inheriting the family business.
Over 30, at loose ends with no fixed job...

But even that's
com-pletely gone now...
to get back up again.
But even then, I'd this
vague assumption that someday, somewhere, I'd get the chance
ゴオオオ
RR
OOO
AAA
RR
?
What's that ?
Snap
Ah, right.
I'll give you all some of this later.

Way back,
when I was in a band in Tokyo,
maybe it was thanks to our music being so extreme,
but we had this one seriously crazy suicidal groupie.
The day the band broke up
she gave me this pendant.
For real ?
I'll split it up for all of us.
There's enough cyanide in here to kill 20 people.
With this, you're sure to croak whenever you want.

How far are we taking him?
I want him to have a place with a nice view, at least.
... Yeah. You're right.
To the summit.

SH.
INK
haa
haa
haa
haa
haa
haa
haa
haa
haa
That hole deep enough ?
Think so.

Internet café
ga & Internet
PitBoy
24h
Pit Boy ...

Nelsin Kato
Authorized Signature
Nelsin Kato-Ricarte
Ricarte.

Slim.
I'm so sorry.

You sold off a kidney just to come to this country
and this is what you got. Sorry.

Doesn't it piss you off?
... Hey.

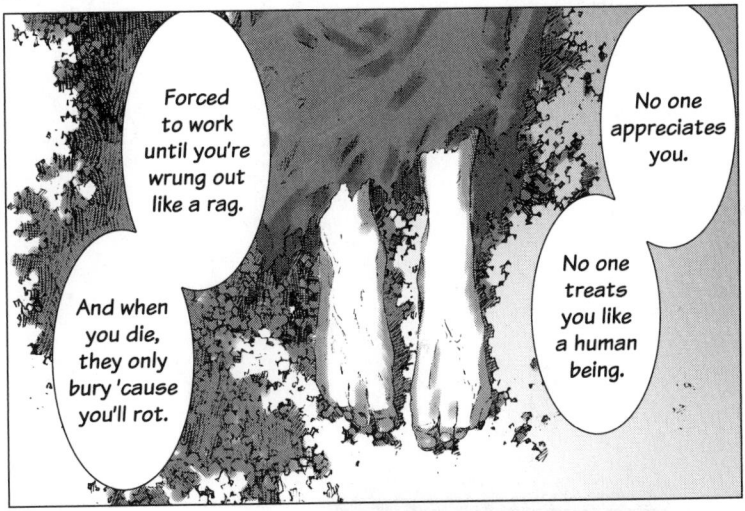
Forced to work until you're wrung out like a rag.
No one appreciates you.
And when you die, they only bury 'cause you'll rot.
No one treats you like a human being.

What are we living for?

...
What are you sayin'?
Fight back ...?
If we go back to the city now, we face life in prison.
Before that, don't you wanna try fighting back as best we can?
No job, no money, no future.
There's nothin' we can do!
... There is.

If we four band together, put our lives on the line,
there's plenty we can do.
888888
BEEP
778912

I have an idea...

PROPHECY
01 END

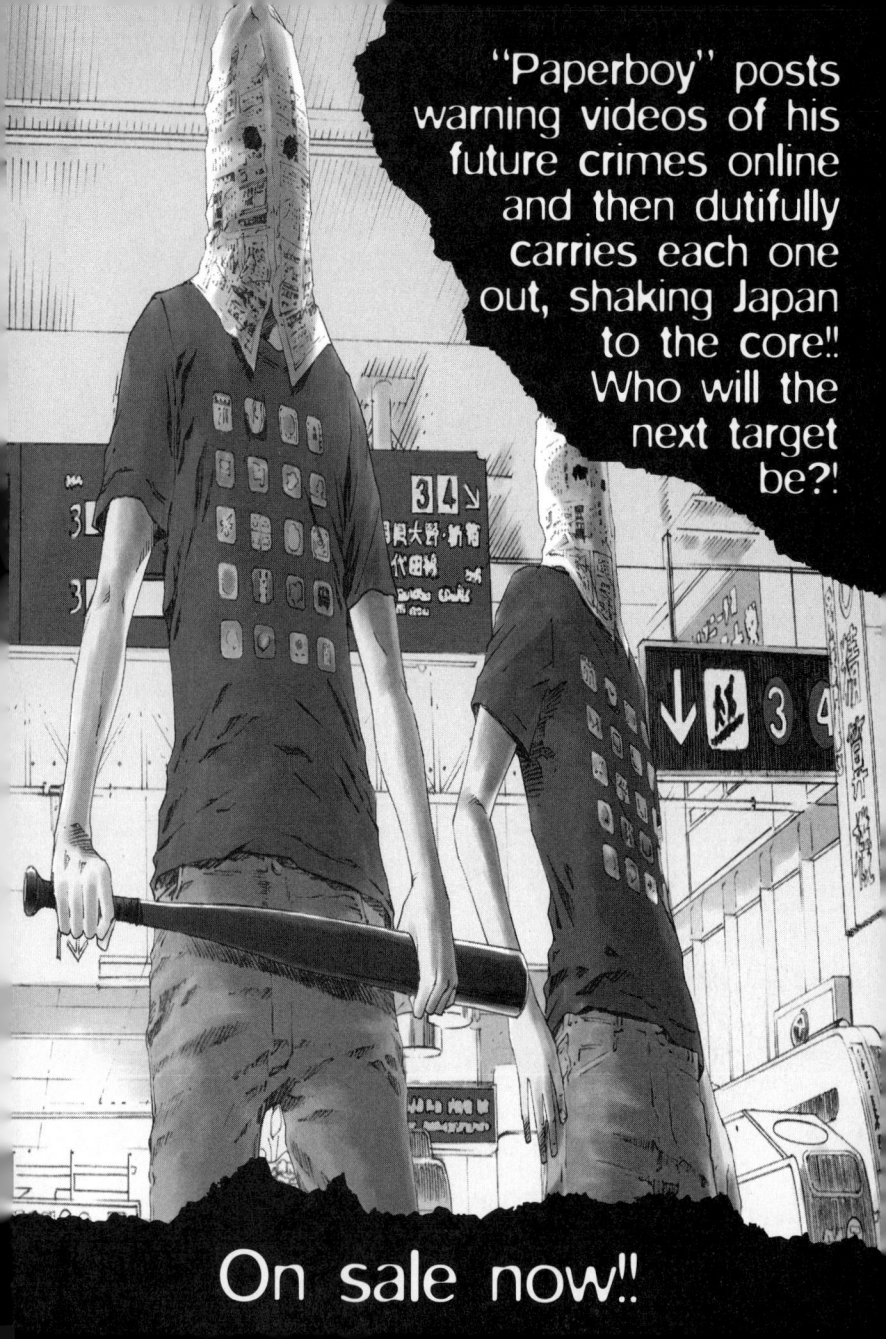
"Paperboy" posts warning videos of his future crimes online and then dutifully carries each one out, shaking Japan to the core!! Who will the next target be?!
On sale now!!

As terrorists in this information-oriented society, just what is their end game ?!
PROPHECY
02 TETSUYA TSUTSUI

AJIN
DEMI-HUMAN

STORY: TSUINA MIURA
ART: GAMON SAKURAI

SAY YOU GET HIT BY A TRUCK AND DIE. YOU COME BACK TO LIFE. GOOD OR BAD?

FOR HIGH SCHOOLER KEI—AND FOR AT LEAST FORTY-SIX OTHERS—IMMORTALITY COMES AS THE NASTIEST SURPRISE EVER.

SADLY FOR KEI, BUT REFRESHINGLY FOR THE READER, SUCH A FEAT DOESN'T MAKE HIM A SUPERHERO. IN THE EYES OF BOTH THE GENERAL PUBLIC AND GOVERNMENTS, HE'S A RARE SPECIMEN WHO NEEDS TO BE HUNTED DOWN AND HANDED OVER TO SCIENTISTS TO BE EXPERIMENTED ON FOR LIFE—A DEMI-HUMAN WHO MUST DIE A THOUSAND DEATHS FOR THE BENEFIT OF HUMANITY.

VOLUMES 1-6 AVAILABLE NOW!

Felipe Smith
PeeloChoo
ALL 3 VOLUMES
AVAILABLE NOW!
FELIPE SMITH
PeeloChoo
VOLUME 1